Friern Barnet

THE LIBRARY

THAT REFUSED TO CLOSE

Keith Martin

Chaville Press
London
2013

Published by Chaville Press

148 Friern Park

London N12 9LU

Copyright © Keith Martin 2013

First published 2013

ISBN 978-0-9569344-7-5

Also by Keith Martin

SKETCHES 1993 to 2011

PEANUTS AT THE TATE – THE CURWEN PRESS –

REMINISCENCES

IRAQ, OTHER SHORT STORIES AND SONGS

WE USED TO WRITE LETTERS

Designed by www.designbycaroline.co.uk

Printed and bound in Great Britain by Jellyfish Print Solutions

THIS BOOK IS DEDICATED

TO THOSE IN THE COMMUNITY

WHO CREATED FRIERN BARNET LIBRARY
IN 1934

AND TO THE TEAM

OF DETERMINED, BRAVE AND
TALENTED PEOPLE

WHO REFUSED FROM 2011 TO 2013

TO LET IT BE CLOSED

Acknowledgements

Thank you, Sarah, for your inspiring Foreword.

The Bloggers of Barnet provide a vein of humour and information which is an essential antidote to the evasiveness that typifies far too much of the pronouncements of some prominent members of Barnet Borough Council. It has even been suggested that the Council will publish a new dictionary, to inform the public, as George Orwell foretold in *Animal Farm*;
'All men are equal, but some are more equal than others',

that there are new meanings in the twenty-first century to words such as

Consultation
Cost effectiveness and
Democracy.

So the author has pleasure in acknowledging the support and enthusiasm of all the bloggers. Those whose contributions appear in this book are

Derek Dishman, alias Mr Mustard
Reema Patel's Blog
Roger Tichborne, who writes Barnet Eye, and
Theresa Musgrove, the redoubtable Mrs Angry of Broken Barnet

This in no way implies anything against the equally incisive blogs of

John Dix, alias Mr Reasonable
La Bloggeuse Devra Kay and
Vicki Morris, Citizen Barnet

This book is designed by Caroline Sloneem. Not just the cover; the whole book. I cannot thank her enough for transforming the pile of newspaper cuttings into what I realize is not a totally legible book, but it would have been a mess without her skill and patience.

The book was originally going to have three co-authors; Rosie Canning, Phoenix and myself. Rosie has instead written a solo version and Phoenix may one day do the same. I wish them well and am grateful to each of them for allowing this volume to include Rosie's minutes of 10 September 2012 and Phoenix's witness statement to the Court. My thanks are due too to Rabbi Jeffrey Newman for permission to reproduce his email from Hungary.

I am very grateful for permission to use the photographs by or obtained from Michael Duke, Vicki Morris, Arnie Donoff and Peter Marshall and Demotix on pages 123, 237, 90 and 236 and to Peter Beal and the copyright holder Hendon Times Newsquest for the photo on page 22.

My grateful thanks also to Sarah Howe, Paul Merchant and Maryla Persak-Enefer, for permission to publish their inspiring artwork on pages 122, 87 and 82 and to the London Borough of Barnet for the image on page 91.

The book would have been incomplete without the press coverage, and I am grateful for this to the publishers and writers of the Daily Mirror, The Guardian, the Morning Star, the London Evening Standard, Sky News, the BBC and the enormously supportive local papers the Ham and High, The Archer, Better Barnet, Barnet Times and Barnet Press.

CONTENTS

ILLUSTRATIONS

FOREWORD

For a number of months in the winter of 2011-12, the Occupy protests outside London's St Paul's became a fixture of my route into work and an inescapable mark on the physical and political landscape of this country. The tent city protests reverberated beyond the hundreds who camped in them and reflected a widespread disaffection with the global social and economic model which had resulted in a financial crisis and economic downturn. As Richard Sennett has written, more than a critique of capitalism, 'the movement's lasting gift is embodied in the very word "occupy"'. The reclaiming of market squares, city parks and the steps of cathedrals reminded us all of their function as public spaces for political expression and social action.

A year later, I found myself speaking in a packed room of Barnet County Court on behalf of the campaigners to save Friern Barnet Library. The relationship between a campaign to save a local library in a leafy corner of North London, where Margaret Thatcher was once the local MP, and a global protest movement may not seem immediately obvious. However, the campaigners' desire to reclaim an important public space resonated beyond its local setting, demonstrating a grassroots thirst for political agency to bring about real social change.

The Library had been closed and was being prepared to be sold to private developers by Barnet Council notwithstanding powerful local opposition. The handsome red-brick building was boarded up and earmarked for sale that is until members of London Occupy entered the empty building. In the weeks which followed, local residents donated thousands of books and contributed many man hours to re-open the Library. Shelves were filled, book lending resumed and classes from English language to pilates were arranged. This dynamic campaign was forged from an unlikely coalition of seasoned Occupy activists and Barnet residents, councillors, pensioners, local business people, single mums, young families and religious leaders. It offered a powerful rebuff to the former MP's declaration that "there is no such thing as society".

However, despite the community's welcoming response to the occupation, the Council pressed on with eviction proceedings to get the campaigners out and the estate agents in.

I became involved as the barrister who advised the campaigners on their legal rights and represented them during the eviction proceedings in court. As a barrister you do hundreds of cases, a handful of which capture your imagination. The challenge to save Friern Barnet Library was one of those cases. Through the collective efforts of the campaigners, the councillors and the legal team and after months of hard work we secured the re-opening of the Library.

The campaign's success was based, in part, on people's emotional identification with the Library as a fixture in community life. Libraries everywhere provide access not only to free books and resources but to a social reality outside the market. As Zadie Smith has written, libraries are one of the few institutions where you don't have to buy anything in order to stay.

The campaign epitomised the "politics of place". Public spaces such as libraries, pubs, museums, places of worship and parks, are part of the fabric of the community and a focus for community activism. These shared spaces are cherished precisely because they are public. In an increasingly privatised, atomised world they provide spaces where strangers can come together, notwithstanding their cultural, social and generational differences, and be bound by their commitment to the community.

A library is a social good which matters to people of different political persuasions. It can, as in Barnet, become a focal point for forging new political alliances. On the face of it, the dreadlocked Occupy activists and the smartly-dressed members of SFBL appeared to have little in common. However, the participation in a protest in defence of a vital public space led to collaboration and lasting social ties which challenged prevailing political stereotypes.

Successful campaigns put people first. Fiona Brickwood, one of the leading campaigners, whose contribution is discussed in these pages told me that she had never thought of herself as a political person before the Library campaign. When she took the witness stand in court, she gave an eloquent defence of what the Library meant to local people. Now Fiona, and all those involved in the campaign have been empowered by the experience of community organising to engage in further activism.

In the following chapters of the "Library that refused to Close" readers have the chance to learn of the dramatic twists and turns of how the library was saved through the hard work and collective efforts of ordinary people. These pages offer an insight into the political and legal strategy, the tactics and the setbacks which culminated on 5 February 2013 in Barnet Council handing over the keys of a library it had closed to a group of community activists it had tried to evict.

Today, Friern Barnet Library is open to everyone. Volunteers are running the library in a public building with some resources from the Council and funds raised by the local community (although more are needed). The campaigners rightly insist that they should be supported by public resources and the knowhow of local government. However, their actions demonstrate that as citizens they are political agents who are more than capable of playing a more active role in the state's activities.

Given its history, it is no surprise that Friern Barnet Library continues to serve as a vibrant community hub and forum for political debate hosting regular classes, lectures and book signings. I am delighted that there is a written record of this inspirational campaign which has reminded us all what grassroots cooperative politics can achieve. I encourage you to visit the Library any day of the week!

Sarah Sackman
August 2013

Sarah was part of the team that saved Friern Barnet Library and represented the library campaigners in court. Sarah practices as a barrister in London specialising in public, planning and environmental law. Her clients include NGOs, local and central government departments and low-income individuals. A graduate of Harvard Law School and Cambridge University, Sarah currently teaches a course at LSE Cities on law and social justice in the city. Sarah is a longstanding volunteer at Toynbee Hall advice centre and has a strong interest in the role of law in grassroots campaigning.

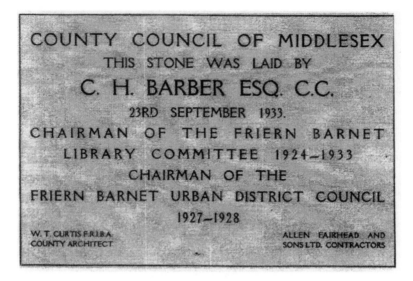

COUNTY COUNCIL OF MIDDLESEX
THIS STONE WAS LAID BY
C. H. BARBER ESQ. C.C.
23RD SEPTEMBER 1933.
CHAIRMAN OF THE FRIERN BARNET
LIBRARY COMMITTEE 1924–1933
CHAIRMAN OF THE
FRIERN BARNET URBAN DISTRICT COUNCIL
1927–1928

W. T. CURTIS F.R.I.B.A.
COUNTY ARCHITECT

ALLEN FAIRHEAD AND
SONS LTD. CONTRACTORS

The foundation stone of Friern Barnet Library, laid on 23 September 1933, six months before it was opened on 23 March 1934

INTRODUCTION

We want our library back.

This in a nutshell was the message that the Save Friern Barnet Library Group was sending to Barnet Council during its long campaign, first to prevent the closure of the library and, after it was summarily closed on 5 April 2012, to get the library reopened.

The campaign painstakingly consulted the local community, built a large following of supporters and petitioned the Council to keep the library open.

To no avail.

Until...on 5 September 2012, some squatters climbed through an open window and invited the community to donate books and join them in running the reopened library.

Now read on.

CHAPTER 1

5 APRIL 2012   THE SIT-IN

Several of the principal characters in this story shared a common experience on 5 April 2012, Maundy Thursday.

One of them, Bill Murphy, was deputed by Barnet Council to remain in the library with those members of the public who chose to stay in the building when it was due to close for lunch at 12 noon. We had received a tip-off that it would not reopen at 1 pm after the lunchtime closure. The Council had announced anyway that this would happen after the official closing time of 4 pm.

The background to this timetable had been a situation brewing for many months. The international recession had its effect on national budgets, hence local budgets and inevitably, as always, cultural activities were vulnerable to cuts when priorities were considered between the cost of essential and less essential services. Some councils made honest efforts to protect their cultural heritage, others – among them Barnet – placed as a higher priority the preservation from increase of Council tax. Councillors repeated as a mantra:

"The status quo is not an option."

Of course the status quo is an option. It must be the starting point to discussion of other options. Probably what they are thinking is that:

"In order to preserve no increase in Council tax, the status quo is not an option."

A budget which values cultural pursuits is an altogether preferable aim to preserving at all costs an unchanged level of Council tax.

My part in all this is as a resident of Friern Barnet since 1965, when Joan and I got married at Hampstead Register Office and purchased a semi-detached house in Friern Park.

Bill Murphy knew, and the fifteen of us knew, that the Council had secretly decided not to reopen it at 1 pm for the afternoon session. This was why the fifteen members of the public remained in place, as a protest against the closure. Bill was one of the new breed of consultants hired by the Council. Not a librarian, he was nevertheless hired on a short-term contract to manage the library staff. He said later that he had visions of spending the whole of   Easter in the company of these stubborn citizens.

But let me begin the day at the beginning.

I keep a pocket 'week to view' diary. That is, seven days cover each two-page spread, so there is room only to remind myself of what I expect to happen.

My entry for 5 April 2012 was:

> 9.30   Kay Gray
>
> FB lib demo + camera
>
> 2.30   Boots

In the event, the fitness class at 9.30 took place as predicted. FB library demonstration went on until 6pm, so I had to borrow a mobile phone from one of the other fifteen demonstrators in the library, to tell Boots Opticians that I needed to reschedule my eye test appointment to another day. This was not the end of the world.

Why was I there that day? Because the library was important to me, and I had heard on the grapevine from Fiona Brickwood that it would be closed at noon.

So, cocooned in the library there were the fifteen protesters, also Bill Murphy together with Chris Palmer, the Assistant Director of something on the Council, and a stern-faced uniformed security guard, one of the army of outsourced services beloved of the Council. Not any one from the library staff, be it noted. Chris was the only one willing to engage in any conversation. He was interested, as am I, in artsdepot, the arts centre at Tally Ho, North Finchley, where I volunteer for four hours a week in the gallery.

Bill was not disposed to reply to questions. I tried to gain his attention.

"Have you read these leaflets on the counter?

'Become a library volunteer. Your library needs you.' That is what we are today, library volunteers."

Bill ignored my question. When one of the female demonstrators asked if she might use the toilet behind the issue desk, she was told "No."

So we found a waste paper bin, which she used behind a library screen. This makeshift WC happened to be in front of the electricity meter and switches, which became apparent when later the Council staff were thwarted in their wish to turn off our access to computer communication with the outside world. By this time the bloggers outside the window were informing the world of the abuse of human rights perpetrated on us by the hapless Bill.

This computer communication, for the computer literate among the fifteen inside, took the form of telephone text messages and tweets, and the dissemination of a Press Release authored jointly by several of our number.   I think I was alone in recording my reportage by hand on paper. I smuggled one such message out of the window to Daniel O'Brien of the Barnet Press.

We could, of course, see the increasingly large multitude of supporters in the side road outside the library. Communication was mainly by telephone and sign language. And, of course, we blue tacked messages on the leaded library windows.

SAVE OUR LIBRARY

- SIT IN

Barnet Council would like us to muffle
Our voices. There's too much kerfuffle.
       But there's need for a change
       And we'd like to arrange
That the cabinet has a reshuffle!

No wonder he's called Mr Toad –
That opponent of humps in the road.
       Wants to privatise parks
       While he wears blings and sparks,
But on May 3 it starts to explode!

(Editor's note

Which it did, of course, with a 26% swing in the Greater London Assembly election against Brian Coleman, the sitting Assembly member and local councillor on Barnet Council . Andrew Dismore, the former Labour MP for Hendon and victorious winner on May 3, was among the army of supporters, journalists and members of the local community outside our cocoon.)

After several hours, some of the well-wishers organised a collection for the purchase of pizzas for the fifteen inside. I must say they tasted good! They were smuggled in through one of the top windows. The library was purpose-built in 1934 with no low windows, in order to avoid draught and papers blowing about. The stern-faced guard (who several months later turned out to be not only human and supportive but a regular supporter of West Ham United!) was hit by a boxed pizza as she mounted guard with her back to the window.

We decided at 6pm, no doubt to the relief of Bill Murphy, not to remain in the library overnight, and were let out of the front door to the acclamation of the assembled public. There were a few celebratory speeches, but we had decided not to sing revolutionary songs. Tirza Waizel, co-ordinator of Barnet Alliance for Public Services and a stalwart campaigner, and I had sung together Leon Rosselson's song (about the Diggers in 1649) The World Turned Upside-down, inside the library, but our fifteen were of various political hues and, after all, a library is a place of quiet...

Shakespeare, as usual, got his oar in before the rest of us. The St Crispin's Day speech in act IV scene iii of Henry V, though the date was six months out, St Crispin being on 25 October:

"He that outlives this day, and comes safe home,
Will stand a tip-toe when this day is named,
And rouse him at the name of Crispian...
Then shall our names,
Familiar in his mouth as household words,
Harry the King, Bedford, and Exeter,

Warwick and Talbot, Salisbury and Gloucester,

Be in their flowing cups freshly rememb'red...

We few, we happy few, we band of brothers...

And gentlemen in England now a-bed

Shall think themselves accursed they were not here,

And hold their manhoods cheap while any speaks

That fought with us upon Saint Crispin's day."

Then shall our names,

Sheri Darby, Fiona Brickwood, Tirza Cohen-Waizel,

Maureen Ivens, Keith Martin, Adam Langleben,

Vicki Morris the Blogger and photographer,

Not to mention those in there with us, equally famous –

Bill Murphy, library manager at Barnet Council,

Chris Palmer, Assistant Director on the Council and willing to talk

rationally about artsdepot,

And those outside smuggling pizzas to us through the high window –

Andrew Dismore, Kath McGuirk, Maryla Persak-Enefer,

Martin Russo, Roger Tichborne,

Andrew Meikle of the Guardian,

Natalie O'Neill of the Barnet Times, Daniel O'Brien of the Press,

Relaying the story and the pictures to the world.

CHAPTER 2

JUNE 2011 TO JUNE 2013

WHAT THE PAPERS SAY

Taking advice from experts

Your story 'Council's library plans ill-conceived' (*Times Series,* June 2) reports Councillor Robert Rams saying he had not heard from any protesters after the demonstration at Friern Barnet Library.

In case my email sent on May 20 did not arrive, I repeat that I cited

■ **Protesters: demonstrate at Friern Barnet Road library**

the role of the library as pioneers in 1934, allowing borrowers free access to bookshelves to select their books.

I said I was sure he had been oblivious to the place of the library in international history, just as he had ignored the heritage of Church Farmhouse Museum and Barnet Museum.

Given his responsibility to the people of Barnet for their cultural heritage and that of their children, it is important he seek the advice of experts in the field, of which Barnet has many, before implementing policies which put at risk irreplaceable parts of our history.

I suggested it was the role of the council to harness this wealth of knowledge and advice for the benefit of us all.

I am sending him a copy of this letter and I can guess there will be many more useful suggestions in the council's library strategy consultation, contributions to which are welcome at all local libraries by June 13.

Keith Martin
Friern Park, North Finchley

eries.co.uk. Please include your nes and/or addresses may be with- e published on the *Times Series*

BARNET TIMES

28 July 2011   Barnet Press

Campaigners and children fail to halt threats to three libraries

Cabinet vote through strategy despite 5,000 objections

By Kim Inam

Residents leaving Barnet Council's cabinet meeting said they were "disappointed" by the decision to axe three libraries.

For almost an hour, residents and local ward councillors pleaded with the senior councillors to rethink plans which include merging Friern Barnet and North Finchley library and relocating Hampstead Garden library.

More than 50 residents attended the meeting at Hendon Town Hall and some questioned the councillors on their plans, which incorporate the merged libraries into a new landmark arts-and-culture library at the artsdepot, in Tally Ho Corner, and relocate book stock from Hampstead Garden library to the Institute Arts Centre next to East Finchley Tube station.

More than 5,000 residents have signed petitions against the proposals.

Ten-year-old Hannah Andrusier asked the cabinet how the closure of Friern Barnet library helps to increase literacy.

She told the councillors: "My twin brother Oscar is in the library every day, so much so the librarians joke they will probably one day lock him in. I go to meet my friends and make new friends there. Where do you think I or my friends will be able to go?"

Council leader Richard Cornelius told her she would be able to make friends at the artsdepot library.

Resident Maureen Ivens highlighted the diverse needs of Friern Barnet. She said: "Any move to close the library would reduce the opportunities for job seekers and will put them at a disadvantage."

John Marshall, councillor for Garden Suburb, defended his ward's library saying: "At the Institute there will not be Rhymetime for children, there won't be computers for students, it's right on the border of the ward so it is not a suitable alternative , especially as parking in the area is so difficult."

Kate Salinger, councillor for Coppetts ward, added: "Everything we have heard is that people of Friern Barnet don't want to lose their library, and why should they? It doesn't cost a lot of money to run. I'm concerned that your minds are made up and that anything I say will fall on deaf ears. You are going through the motions of democracy – some of you don't even look like you're listening.

"Our council is a Conservative one, and as such we should conserve what's good. We believe in localism, so why don't we treasure and preserve what's local?

"People are giving us a waste disposal site, we don't want that. We do want our library."

But despite the representations the cabinet voted through the strategy, with a concession of allowing community groups to come forward with alternative proposals for their local libraries before the end of October. In reaction, Hannah said: "They don't give an answer that was worth anything. It's not what you expect from people who should be helping you."

Her father Tim Redmond added: "She asked a straightforward question and got a nonsensical answer. "

Student Kim Lee, who helped organise the campaign to protect Friern Barnet library, including a protest earlier this month, added: "Our campaign won't just suddenly go away, we will look at possible options to how we can save our library."

Robert Rams, cabinet member for partnerships, told The Press he believed the cabinet's decision had secured the future of the service for the next decade.

He said: "Library services are declining across London – we are not doing that in Barnet. We have listened and offered those in Friern Barnet and Hampstead Garden Suburb to come forward with a community use for the building or a facility in the area. Friary House is an example we could use. It was bequeathed to the council and lots of community groups work there. At the top there are three wonderful-sized rooms not currently being used. They could propose to move the stock in there for the community to run. That's one of many options, we need not be tied to one building."

Mr Rams admitted the council has a lease on Hampstead Garden library until 2016, but says the plans would save £375,000. The council will now draw up a memorandum of understanding with the artsdepot board. He added: "We will move as quickly as possible, we have to make sure the gap in provision is weeks rather than months."

4 August 2011   Barnet Press

Ruling Group must be brought to book

Kim Inam's report of the recent Barnet Cabinet meeting (July 28) shows how far removed the current ruling majority on Barnet Council is from reality – or the wishes of the general public – as it lost all the arguments at the meeting.

1   Councillor Rams lost on points in public debate to the good sense of a ten-year-old schoolgirl.

2   The majority of voting councillors refused to listen to the brave and eloquent arguments of two Conservative colleagues in Kate Salinger and former MP John Marshall. As Kate put it, they were merely going through the motions of democracy.

3   They ignored the considerable weight of public opinion shown in the recent library consultation.

4   There was a puzzled lack of comprehension about the quotes from Councillor Robert Rams. He spoke of the many options for the future of libraries but failed to address the one being advanced most strongly – and the least expensive – that of preserving the status quo and keeping good libraries open. Then he actually dared to

add: 'We have to make sure the gap in provision is weeks rather than months.'

Would British Gas, if faced with transferring power from one source of supply to another, actually plan for a gap and leave everyone without light and heat?

This is what he is saying.

I can only presume that the stay of execution proposed until October 31 is a misprint and should read October 31, 2012. Negotiations with artsdepot have scarcely started, and clearly a new library cannot be up and running in three months – the deadline he gives before planning to leave thousands of the population in limbo with no libraries at all.

Let's have a clear statement that there will be no change from the status quo for at least fifteen months. This will give everyone time to consider the options.

Keith Martin

Friern Park, North Finchley

What's On in the Borough

Diary of Events by BBAC's 100 member societies.
Barnet Borough Arts Council is an independent charity.

BARNET ARTS

Winter 2011–2012
www.barnetarts.org.uk

ANY ANSWERS?

FRIERN BARNET LIBRARY

Questions have been raised on the future of Friern Barnet Library where notice of closure has been given. The organisers of protests were given three months in which to present an alternative scheme, which they are now presenting. A decision from the Borough Council is awaited.

The proposal from the Borough Council is that operations be transferred to arts depot's building where a regional library should be created which could also incorporate North Finchley library, but there is no indication as to whether this will indeed take place or when it would do so. Members of Friern Barnet Library are concerned that their building may be closed before alternative arrangements are in place.

It is to be hoped that a scheme can be worked out for Friern Barnet Library, perhaps similar to that put forward by Barnet Museum which has been accepted in principal, and where only the final requirements of the lease have still to be settled. Both schemes rely heavily on assistance by volunteers, but similar schemes are working satisfactorily in other parts of Britain.

ARTS DEPOT

Whether the proposal to add a library into arts depot is feasible is not known. A detailed assessment made in 2004 on possible alternative use as a library when the building was unfinished concluded that it was best used for its intended purpose of the presentation of live arts – with theatres and a gallery space.

CHURCH FARMHOUSE MUSEUM

In the meantime local societies have been trying to find out what is happening to Church Farmhouse Museum building following its closure at the end of March. Questions were raised at a recent Council meeting on whether inventories have been taken and storage facilities arranged.

The answer by Cllr Robert Rams was
"The operating budget for Church Farm museum remains in place as the building still belongs to the Council and must be maintained until alternative uses are agreed. The collection is currently stored in the building. There is therefore no specific additional cost incurred by storing the collection. The building is closed to the public. No other items from the collection have been removed except where loan items are being returned to lenders. An inventory of items returned to lenders is not yet available as this action is not yet complete"

Our members will be hoping that the inventory will be available soon.

ANY ANSWERS ?

From: Keith Martin [mailto:keith.martin18@btinternet.com]

Sent: 25 November 2011 06:14

To: Barnet Press (letters.barnet@nlhnews.co.uk)

Subject: ANY ANSWERS?

Dear Sir

Barnet Arts Winter 2011-2012, the newsletter of Barnet Borough Arts Council, carries the headline "Any Answers?", and asks this question to Barnet Council over its plans for Friern Barnet Library, artsdepot and Church Farmhouse Museum.

The Council announced its budget strategy for cuts of £43m over three years the day after it received news of the £27m windfall from Icelandic banks, thus too late to revise publication of the budget. However, the timetable of public consultations and meetings to approve the budget, and the strategy itself, clearly requires amendment to take account of Barnet's plans for using this windfall.

Starting with the three questions posed by Barnet Arts, the Council must come clean, and put out to public consultation, its revised budget for Friern Barnet library, artsdepot and Church Farmhouse

Museum. The old premise of requiring to raise £3m from selling museums and libraries is clearly out-of-date.

At the same time, so that the strategy is reviewed as a whole, the public requires to know the revised plans for Children's and youth services, grants to Age UK Barnet and other local organizations, what used to be the Arts Department, car parking charges, and Town Hall staff salaries currently frozen.

Any consultation, let alone any decisions, must reflect current circumstances and would otherwise be meaningless. Any answers please?

Keith Martin

148 Friern Park

Follow stars by signing petition

Call to reopen library

Last month, Natalie O'Neill reported the progress of the petition instigated by Rosie Canning to reopen Friern Barnet library ('Bookish actors and authors sign petition' *Times Series,* May 3).

The signatories included Prunella Scales and Timothy West, on their visit to an evening of poetry at the artsdepot, as well as the authors David Nicholls and Paolo Hewitt.

You also published an interview with Miriam Margolyes by Rosy Moorhead ('Meeting the women in Dickens's life', *Times Series,* June 14),

Following her sell-out evening at the artsdepot, Miriam added her autograph to the petition.

To sign the petition, which is open to everyone regardless of where they live, one can also visit www.petitions.barnet.gov.uk.

Olympic exhibition

What should be on show

The documentary film A Tale of Two Barnets will be shown at the Edinburgh International Film Festival next month.

The film shows interviews with residents affected by current Barnet Council policies, together with comments by the leader of the council and its chief executive officer.

Meanwhile Barnet library service, together with artsdepot, has obtained National Lottery funding for what promises to be an attractive exhibition of local images from 1908 and 1948, (when the London Olympic Games included water polo in Finchley Lido).

It will be shown together with current recordings of people's emotions and thoughts on 2012.

Councillor Robert Rams says the project will show how the borough played its part in this Olympic year.

The exhibition should include clips from A Tale of Two Barnets, and reports from the *Times Series*.

The borough is continuing to play its part by closing museums and libraries, unless the wave of public opinion currently rocking the council succeeds in reopening them.

Now that would be something for us all to celebrate.

Keith Martin
Friern Park, Friern Barnet

The recent popularity of Friern Barnet People's Library, which has been a social success under a marquee of a Saturday morning on the green outside the closed library, and was featured with Melvyn Bragg on The One Show on BBC 1, serves to emphasise to the philistines on the cabinet of Barnet Council, who closed the library, that the swell of public opinion for reopening it is something that will not go away until it does a U-turn and puts the community first for a change.

Keith Martin

Friern Park

Friern Barnet.

BARNET PRESS

Thursday, July 5, 2012   www.northlondon-today.co.uk

Twitter @NrthLondonNews

Campaigners want library to be awarded historic building status

By Daniel O'Brien

AN ARCHITECT has asked planning chiefs to add Friern Barnet Library to its list of historic buildings.

Maria Persak-Enefer, of Dale Green Road, Finchley, has submitted a 98-page document to the council's heritage team arguing that the library building should be recognised locally for its architectural and historical heritage.

The library in Friern Barnet Road was controversially closed on April 5 as part of a merger with North Finchley Library, in a new landmark arts library at artsdepot, in Tally Ho Corner.

Members of the Save Friern Barnet Library campaign group had been lobbying Barnet Council since the cabinet voted through its library strategy last July.

The dossier, submitted last month, includes an account of the library's history by Dorrell Dressekie, of the Friern Barnet And District Local History Society, and an assessment of the building's architectural and community value by local campaigner Dr Oliver Natelson.

Mrs Persak-Enefer said: "The library is part of the core of Friern Barnet and it's very important it stays as a part of it."

Campaigners have so far been unsuccessful in their attempts to have the

building, which opened in 1934, listed with English Heritage.

A local listing would not afford the building the same statutory protection from development.

However, council guidelines state that it should be the authority's intention to preserve and enhance these listed buildings where possible.

Dr Natelson, who was recognised last month for his commitment to protecting natural and historical sites, said the

building had all the qualities to make it on to the council list.

The Observer's Unsung Local Hero award winner said: "It was the first building in Middlesex to be specifically designed to be a library.

"But it is not just a library – it is a meeting place for the community."

A council spokeswoman told The Press that the authority was considering the request.

daniel.obrien@nlhnews.co.uk

From left, activists Dorrell Daessekie, Maria Persak-Enefer and Oliver Natelson outside Friern Barnet Library

24 July 2012   Better Barnet

Let's keep it up!

posted by Keith Martin

The march on Saturday 21 July against Barnet Council's One Barnet programme of outsourcing was an inspiring reminder of the spirit of the local community. The sun shone, the atmosphere was positive, there was co-operation from the cheerful police escort, and especially there was a sense of purpose in the joint effort of Barnet Alliance for Public Services (BAPS), the Save Friern Barnet Library Group, Barnet Unison, the GMB and all their supporters.

The happy team was typified by BAPS activist Tirza Waisel's masterly handling of Barnet's petty threat to fine the organizers up to £20,000 for playing music in Victoria Park after the rally. This was avoided by Helen Michael's invitation for us to go to Café Buzz instead, and have music there.

Roger Tichborne (of Barnet Eye fame) let me sing a few songs as well as the booked groups. I introduced

> I'm gonna walk with Nick Walkley (clap, clap)
> Down by the riverside

by asking what it was that BAPS and trade unions do much better than Barnet Council?

ORGANIZE!

Tirza Waisel from Barnet Alliance for Public Services wrote afterwards:

Thanks for a great day and a successful parade. Many, many thanks to all who took on the hard work of the last few weeks.
It has been a huge pleasure for me personally to work with so many dedicated, wise, hard-working activists. And the result – a fantastic community action with a brilliant atmosphere and fun and, most importantly, a strong and clear message to the councillors.

Cost of loaning out each book at interim library around £40

Barnet Council scrutiny committee is a welcome place where councillors are encouraged to follow their consciences.

They did so in recommending that Friern Barnet Library remains open as the decision to close it was flawed.

It was the cabinet which overruled the recommendation and closed the library, calling into question its own integrity.

At another scrutiny committee last week, Rosie Canning, leading a large petition to reopen the library, addressed the cabinet.

Among the facts revealed is that rough estimates of the cost per loan of books from the new interim library at artsdepot put it at about £40 per loan – clearly a wasteful use of resources and money. Rent of £30,000 per year and staffing and other costs, say £20,000, add up to about £1,000 per week.

Books borrowed average a meagre 25 per week, hence £40 per loan.

Progress? We don't think so

YOUR interview with council leader Richard Cornelius was published in the same issue as Alison Moore's salutary reminder that "the Conservative council seems determined to sell Barnet's services and community facilities to the highest bidder" (The Press, August 9).

This gives the lie to his reckless plans for outsourcing.

In an interview in The Press a year ago, Councillor Cornelius said: "We should always go back to the beginning and question why we are doing something."

The leader of Barnet Council has the responsibility to influence decisions which will bind residents and trades people of Barnet to large and long-term contracts with a common purpose of creating profit for outside corporations at the expense of the council.

He is aware that he is ignoring the advice which has persuaded more than 300 other councils in the UK not to make similar calamitous decisions, but fails to mention this.

Barnet received the wisdom of Helen Michael, the chairman of North Finchley traders, when she addressed them as the instigator of a petition from more than 13,000 people asking it to change parking policies responsible for many traders going out of business. This is not an insignificant number of petitioners.

Mr Cornelius owes an apology to Helen Michael for his insulting dismissal of her sound advice in the following statement:

"The North Finchley parking review is also under way, so we should know what all the traders think, rather than just those who are most vocal. I think it is important to know what the shopkeepers actually want."

But 13,000 petitioners have told you that already. They want people to be able to pay cash at parking meters, just like in the car park at The Spires.

The council is elected to serve the people and put the community first, not multinational businesses.
Keith Martin
Friern Park, Friern Barnet

❏ RICHARD CORNELIUS says that he believes he has made progress in his first year, but I think he must be in denial.

One Barnet outsourcing is running behind schedule and millions of pounds over budget on consultancy costs.

He has presided over the closure of Friern Barnet Library, which could have been kept open at a much reduced cost if the council had accepted the community proposals for running the library.

Day centres have closed and the most vulnerable are struggling financially with the ironically named "fairer contributions policy".

The park private hire policy has been pushed through in those areas that didn't complain in sufficient numbers.

Parking is a mess, the Hendon Football Club site sale subject to a judicial review, lots of suppliers still don't have proper contracts with the council and residents are still forbidden to discuss anything that relates to policy or planning at residents' forums.

I'm sorry, Councillor Cornelius, but the last year has been a disaster and that is down to you.
John Dix
Pymmes Brook Drive, Barnet

❏ COUNCILLOR Cornelius may well describe himself as a "natural conservative", so why is he backing the sort of Conservatism that divides society and deliberately cuts and abolishes services that help the most disadvantaged and opposes any sort of collective provision?

It is one thing to have to cut services for financial reasons, it is another entirely to dismantle local government for your own, very political, very right-wing ends.
David Beere
Colin Crescent, Colindale

One would presume that a sound management would demand a swift end to such unnecessary extravagance and a very welcome return of the comprehensive and cost-effective service offered at Friern Barnet.

This library should be reopened immediately and the interim one closed as a costly failure.

Keith Martin
Friern Park
Friern Barnet

23 August 2012   Barnet Press

Public views ignored over library closures

There is a brazen consistency in Councillor Robert Rams's reaction to public criticism. He ignores it.

When the council audit committee reprimanded him for his tardiness in beginning to negotiate with artsdepot for the introduction of a landmark library at Tally Ho Corner and the scrutiny committee recommended that Friern Barnet Library be kept open, his reaction was summarily to close the library and deprive schoolchildren of a place to revise for their exams.

Recently, he wrote individually to residents who had signed the petition to reopen the library, his message blithely ignoring the repeated recommendation of a second scrutiny committee to reconsider the closure.

He said: 'In response to requests, the council has agreed an interim library at Tally Ho Corner, as we work hard to develop plans for a landmark library at artsdepot.

'Although we have been asked to reopen the Friern Barnet library building, no one has come up with a robust alternative to the saving we need to make to meet the budget set for the service by the full council.'

This is the fundamental flaw in the whole argument. The Conservative budget does not put the community first. Try the alternative budget proposed by the Labour Party group, and you will find that most of your self-imposed difficulties will disappear.

Keith Martin

Friern Park
Friern Barnet

Choices exist, but must be made wisely

The debate about culture in Barnet and about the outsourcing of public services has had the positive effect of alerting the electorate to the differing attitudes of the political right and left, and the contrasting choices available to the people of Barnet.

The good news is we have a choice.

For the future cultural heritage of our children, it is between the Philistine policies of the Conservatives on the council, who have closed museums and libraries and withdrawn core funding from artsdepot, and all other councillors, who support the efforts of the majority of artists, writers and educationalists in Barnet.

The debate on public services is equally clear. We can choose the One Barnet programme of outsourcing to big business, already abandoned as a costly failure by the majority of councils in the country which have tried it and found it wanting.

Or we can choose to support the policies advocated by Barnet Alliance for Public Services, of real consultations with the community, of real democracy within the council chamber and exercise of each councillor's individual choice, and of harnessing the expertise of qualified and experienced people of goodwill in Barnet to give their advice to council committees and help to choose appropriate ways of managing public services for the benefit of all citizens.

Keith Martin

Friern Park

Friern Barnet

Squatters reopen London library

Diane Taylor

A few dog-eared copies of novels by Joanna Trollope and Wilbur Smith sit on the otherwise bare shelves of Friern Barnet library alongside banners urging "peace", "occupy" and "revolution". The library closed down by Barnet council in April is under new management.

Eight squatters entered the London library last week through an open window. Since a law change on 1 September made it a criminal offence to squat residential properties, they have turned to commercial properties to find a bed for the night. The occupation has the blessing of many residents who are delighted to see the locked doors of the library flung open.

Council officials have been trying for months to persuade locals to become volunteer librarians in a room in a nearby council building instead. The proposal has not been well received and stalemate has prevailed.

All that changed when the squatters moved in and embarked on negotiations with senior council officials who were invited to the library on Monday to meet the new occupants. Another meeting has been scheduled for next week.

Yesterday the squatters, who describe themselves as caretakers, opened for business, lending books for the first time since the council closed the library.

A Barnet council spokeswoman said: "We are still continuing conversations with the protesters but at the same time the council has started the legal process to have the occupants removed."

THE GUARDIAN 12 SEPT 2012 page 6

Squatters 'to reopen London library closed in council cuts'

Rob Parsons

SQUATTERS have occupied a north London library five months after it was closed down as part of council cost-cutting moves.

The group said they "invaded" empty Friern Barnet Library through an open window and have set themselves up as "community librarians".

They claim they will reopen the library, which was closed by Barnet council in April, for 16 hours a week while a decision is made over its future. Eight squatters entered last week, though today only three were sleeping inside. Some moved in after a law change this month made it a criminal offence to squat in residential properties.

One of the squatters, Dan, 31, a Hungarian previously involved in the occupation of Old Street magistrates' court this year, claimed they want to save the building from demolition.

He said: "Libraries are cultural hubs, there are lots of reasons why people need them. People need to read books – even in the age of the internet, libraries are really crucial."

The library closure followed a campaign by local residents opposed to plans for a merger with North Finchley library. As part of Barnet council's

efforts to save £1.4 million from its library budget, it plans to create a new "landmark library" based at Artsdepot in North Finchley.

The squatters, who include students, artists and a former librarian, plan to reopen the building on Tuesdays, Wednesdays, Thursdays and Saturdays between 11am and 3pm.

In a notice posted outside, the occupiers said they had "links with several groups and have begun negotiations with Barnet council". They have already acquired 400 books and have started lending them out. Dan said: "Some friends of ours got in and realised this place was important, so they got in contact with us and our friends.

"For us it was about opening up the library. We saw it was really important for local people. They have been trying for 18 months with protests and petitions and have been hitting brick walls,

so we thought some direct action could build a bridge with the council."

A council spokeswoman said the authority is committed to seeing the squatters removed from the building and has started legal action.

She added that talks are being held about the possibility of the group opening a community library in empty Friary House at Friary Park.

London faces major public library closures because of spending cuts.

Lending support a squatter known as Phoenix at Friern Barnet library. His group plans to open a "community library" there

LONDON EVENING STANDARD 12 SEPT 2012

Library squatters face legal action

BARNET TIMES SEPT 13 2012

by CHRIS HEWETT
chewett@london.newsquest.co.uk

Legal action has been started to remove squatters who have taken control of the closed Friern Barnet Library.

Activists broke into the building, in Friern Barnet Road, last week and have opened their own community library.

However, the group has been in negotiations with Barnet Council for more than a week about setting up the facility permanently.

Council officers want to move the group to the empty Friary House, in Friary Park, but the protesters have won support from several community groups, including campaigners who fought to keep the library open.

The popular facility was shut down in April, as a cost-cutting measure by Barnet Council, which is looking to sell the land.

The authority is paying more than £600 a day for security staff to monitor the building around the clock and £120 a month to keep gas and electricity running.

The council has come under fire over its handling of the situation after its deputy chief executive and two senior library officers entered into negotiations with the group, last Wednesday.

Maureen Ivens, chairman of the Save Friern Barnet Library group, said in a statement: "This is surely the most absurd action by the council in the saga of the closure of Friern Barnet Library.

"Rather than simply reopen our desperately needed library, they are willing to collude in a civil offence — all to save face."

Under squatting laws, it could take the council up to a month to remove the activists.

One of the occupiers, Pete Phoenix, said the group was working on a rotation basis of dozens of people who would open the library for up to three days a week.

The 41-year-old said he was amazed by the level of engagement by the council.

He said: "It has been extraordinarily co-operative. I've been doing this for 20 years and have never known a council to do this before."

Fiona Brickwood has been in talks with the council for a year over plans to open up a youth skills training centre in the former library.

She said: "There are some peculiar things going on. If someone has broken into your building — a criminal offence — you don't walk them down to another one and offer that instead."

A council representative said it was genuinely enthusiastic about any group proposing ideas for a community library at Friary House, but added: "However, it is important public assets are protected and we have now started the legal process to have the squatters removed."

■ **Squatters, including Pheonix, left, open Friern Barnet Library to visitors**
Picture NL32494 by John Macdonald-Fulton

Friern Barnet Library

Wise words to find a solution

At the court hearing for the eviction of the occupants of Friern Barnet library, who have been using their tenure to reopen the library to the community and negotiate a permanent solution with Barnet Borough Council, the judge outlined his recommendations.

These were that the two sides to the dispute should get together to try to resolve their differences with, if necessary, the aid of a mediator.

If this should prove difficult, he built in the possibility of the case going to trial between December 17 and 21.

The council response has been to reject the judge's recommendation to resume a dialogue with the occupants.

I have a personal conflict of interest in the matter. I am a co-defendant with Phoenix and the occupants and am a long-term Barnet resident.

As such, I am critical of the council's stance in continuing to waste public money on expensive legal costs when it is being offered an opportunity to discuss matters and reach a solution acceptable to both sides.

There are several bodies trying to broker a resolution to this matter.

One is the Save Friern Barnet Library Group; another is Barnet Borough Arts Council (BBAC). I am a member of both.

BBAC has a scheme for reopening both the library and Church Farmhouse Museum, in Hendon, which envisages a partnership between eight partners – including the council, Arts Council England, English Heritage, Hendon and District Archaeological Society (HADAS), the London Heritage Lottery Fund, and the New Carnegie Foundation. (Editor's note: see Appendix I 23.10.12, page 255).

I am appealing to the leader of the council, Councillor Richard Cornelius, to grasp the window of opportunity recommended by the court.

Keith Martin

Friern Park
Friern Barnet

Book signing

Umbrella by **Will Self** was published in August this year and shortlisted for the 2012 Man Booker prize. Set in Friern Barnet mental hospital, it is a magnificent piece of modernist prose about the first world war and mental illness

Wednesday 14 November, 7pm, free event at Friern Barnet community library

A rare chance to meet one of Britain's leading authors at this reading, book signing and discussion

Journalist, novelist, thinker, broadcaster, intellectual satirist, professor of contemporary thought *'He is one of those rare writers whose imaginations change for ever the way we see the world'*
- JG Ballard

UMBRELLA

WILL SELF

WITH TORY CUTS CLOSING 8 LIBRARIES A MONTH ROS WYNNE-JONES VISITS ONE FIGHTING BACK

The rise of the guerilla library

WALK into Friern Barnet Library in North London and you would think you were standing in a model public library.

More than 1,000 fiction, non-fiction and children's titles are stacked neatly on shelves.

There are comfy armchairs, three computer terminals linked up to the internet and friendly librarians making helpful recommendations.

There's a DVD and CD section and a kids' area. Pilates and children's singing groups abound. It's warm, and the carpets and toilets are spotless.

Tonight, author Will Self is doing a reading from his book Umbrella, nominated for the Man Booker prize.

"You'd want to congratulate the local council on a brilliant service," says a pensioner on her way to use the free internet facilities.

"Only it's not the council who are running it. It's the people."

Friern Barnet Library was closed down earlier this year by Barnet Council, a Conservative-run London borough with a fierce cuts policy.

Its "One Barnet" strategy involves outsourcing nearly everything the council currently does – resulting in up to £1billion of contracts. "Now the

▲ WELL READ Author Keith Martin

library is being run by renegade librarians," confides the pensioner. "It's very exciting."

On April 5, after 78 years keeping the local community informed and entertained, the library was closed with just 24 hours' notice. Every book and every stick of furniture gone.

Some of the locals staged an impromptu sit-in.

"We sat down in the building for six hours," says 74-year-old author Keith Martin, who has lived in the area for 47 years.

"They wouldn't let us use the toilet, which was outrageous, but a local pizza company passed some pizzas in through the window."

It was the start of the community coming together. A pop-up library opened on the green outside, with hundreds of people browsing books under gazebos. A petition gathered more than 3,000 names in support.

Then on September 5, the building was "reopened" by Occupy – the non-violent demonstrators responsible for the St Paul's Cathedral protest. The local residents did the rest.

"Guerilla librarian," smiles local mum Rona De Souza, 44.

"I suppose that's what I am. I love volunteering here. My kids and I were devastated when it closed down. Then one day we walked past and saw it was open again. We came in and now we're helping out.

"My 13-year-old daughter helped get the fiction shelf in alphabetical order.

"I've brought along a copy of JK Rowling's new book, but it turns out they need shelves more than books.

"We've got so many duplicate books we're giving them away in

return for donations to keep the heating and lighting on," Rona says.

Keith is less than diplomatic about the closure. He says: "The council are philistines. One of the councillors said we didn't need libraries now, you can do everything at Starbucks."

A chain cafe looked to be the likely fate of the building. Residents also feared a supermarket or a new

block of flats. Occupy member Leon, 28, says they are not at the library with any hidden agenda.

"This isn't about squatting," he says. "We're not here for a place to stay. We haven't provided the books, the furniture, the librarians. The local community have done it all."

Local Labour councillor Barry Rawlings agrees. "When people squat they usually lock themselves in," he says. "This is the opposite. They are

here to open the doors." The council has twice been to court to have the renegades evicted and time has been set aside for a decision in December.

The activists even have a name for their adversary – EasyCouncil.

"It's trying to be a no-frills council, cutting everything back," Barry says. "But it isn't just running a business, it should be much more than that."

If you look carefully you can see tiny clues to the library's new identity. A handwritten rota up on the wall. Volunteers making tea in the kitchen. The emergency instructions if the police or bailiffs should come.

> ### People look at what we're doing here and want their public spaces open too
> OCCUPY ACTIVIST

"We still believe we can negotiate our way out of this," says Martin Russo, 43, chair of Save Friern Barnet Library. "We still hope we can find a way to get our library back."

Of course, libraries are about more than just books. They are deeply personal to their members.

Alfred Ruringewa, a Rwandan refugee, says: "When I came to this country, this place was everything to me. I had five children and I was a single father.

"I used to leave them here to do their homework and the ladies of the library would look after them and see that they were safe while I went to the supermarket after work.

"Now my daughter Diane is in her third year studying criminology.

"My son is going to the University of Kent to study psychology. My other children are doing well.

GENOCIDE

"All my books were destroyed in the Rwandan genocide. Imagine my joy when I discovered them here again, the Latin and Greek texts I had studied at school. I will never, ever forget that day."

He falls silent for a moment, then adds: "So yes, you could say this library is important to me."

Barnet Council say it is continuing with legal proceedings because it "has a duty to its taxpayers to protect its assets... this will mean we cannot have any further discussions about a community library until the court case is finished."

In the meantime: "The council does not accept liability for any events taking place within the former Friern Barnet Library building."

It is the politest of revolutions, run on little more than strong tea, plain biscuits, an internet connection and a healthy dose of idealism.

But to communities that have been cut beyond what they can bear, it is also a template.

"We have had messages from all over the country," says Leon.

"People are looking at what we're doing here and they want us to come and open up their public spaces too. This is just the start."

PEOPLE POWER Helpers at Friern Barnet

BOOKISH Our Ros reads up

FULLY BOOKED Friern Barnet Library and rota

Friern Barnet Library

Tory group like scared rabbits

At the meeting of Barnet Borough Council on November 6, the Conservative Group went to elaborate extremes to avoid a debate on Friern Barnet Library.

The members were as paralysed as rabbits in the spotlight of criticism. They are running scared at the self-imposed dilemma presented by their continued advocacy of committing the borough to risky ten-year terms for outsourcing major contracts for public services.

By using the current majority on the council to bulldoze through these plans, all they will achieve — when the inevitable claims come in from outsourcing firms and the promised surpluses turn into massive deficits — is to send to the electorate a message never to allow them to return to power in Barnet.

At least, not until the effect has worn off, way beyond the year 2023.

An interesting comment to your letters on October 25 from the leader of the council ('Duty to spend money wisely') and myself ('Wise Words Find a Solution', *Your Views*): the lady who delivers the *Times Series* in my road reads the letters page and knocked on my door last Thursday.

"You're going to win, aren't you, about reopening the library?" she said. "How many copies would you like?"

I replied that I thought she might get evens at Ladbrokes for Friern Barnet Library to be officially reopened by this Christmas.

Keith Martin
Friern Park, Friern Barnet

National

Tories divided over Barnet's 'easyCouncil' outsourcing plan

Robert Booth

Fresh cracks have appeared in the Conservatives' resolve to drive through one of Britain's most controversial programmes of local authority cuts.

Leaked emails have revealed a bitter internal dispute about whether the party has any mandate to drive through outsourcing for more than £500m in contracts under the "easyCouncil" programme to provide no-frills council service. Barnet's programme has been seen as a testbed for wholesale cuts in the provision of public services by councils but this week the local Conservative MP Matthew Offord and the Conservative councillor Sury Khatri engaged in an angry row over the party's right to push through cuts.

"The Conservative party did not campaign on this basis and we do not have a mandate, Khatri told Offord, according to leaked emails seen by the Guardian. "None of the literature we distributed prior to the election mentioned one iota of this. The local people do not want this and have not been consulted, hence the vociferous reaction by residents. As councillors, we still have no details on this so how can we have campaigned that this was the best thing since sliced bread."

Offord had drafted a letter to mollify residents who had complained about the cuts, insisting the council was elected on a mandate to push through the imminent outsourcing of contracts to private firms such as BT, Capita and EC Harris.

A £275m contract is due to be outsourced on 6 December and another estimated to be worth up to £750m will be awarded early next year. They will hand over responsibility to the private sector for the running of building control, planning, highways and transport, the crematorium and cemetery, trading standards, licensing and environmental health.

Khatri insisted Offord's claim that voters knew what was coming was "misleading". "Am sorry to say I disagree," Khatri wrote. "WE DO NOT HAVE A MANDATE." "What details were available then so how can a resident say he agrees with when they voted for the Conservatives?"

wrote Khatri. "Can you tell me how we had publicised this fact? As I did not come across any material on this when we were campaigning for election. As of today we still do not have any details."

The exchange comes as the council's outsourcing faces a series of crises.

John Sullivan and his disabled daughter, Susan, have begun judicial review

> 'The local people do not want this and have not been consulted'
>
> Sury Khatri, Barnet councillor

proceedings against the council over concerns at what privatisation means for the care of adults with disabilities.

Brian Coleman, the councillor responsible for parking, had the Tory whip withdrawn after he was charged with assault and careless driving. He then turned on the plan, urging the council "to dump One Barnet and return to core local government values and make sure this particular turkey does not see Christmas!"

Earlier this month, the council leader, Richard Cornelius, survived a no-confidence vote and in October, the chief executive, Nick Walkley, who was responsible for devising the programme, resigned unexpectedly to join the neighbouring Labour-controlled Haringey council.

29 November 2012   Barnet Times

Friern Barnet Library
Judgement day for community

On the agenda for the Barnet Borough Council cabinet resources committee meeting on December 17, is a proposal to seek permission to commence the marketing of Friern Barnet Library in order to dispose of it, ('Spoiling the plot', *Barnet and Borough Times,* November 22).

This astonishing council-inspired idea seems to me to be ignoring the following:

There is a law against contempt of court. The process of eviction of the occupants may have been heard in court on the very day and may not have reached a judgement.

The library was reopened by the occupants on September 5, to the delight of the community, who have donated their time and more than 6,000 books towards running it.

Richard Cornelius, the Leader of the Council, does not appear to be in touch with his colleagues or staff. Nor did he reply to my invitation to come as my guest to the vibrant evening at the library with Will Self.

Nor has he yet replied to my invitation to visit the library at a less crowded moment, to experience for himself the inspiration of such an active and valued library.

What is the purpose of having an elected council if it ignores its duties to those whom it represents?

Keith Martin

Friern Park
Friern Barnet

OPINION | letters@hamhigh.co.uk

Follow us online at
www.hamhigh.co.uk

Councillors

Public servants or our masters

Keith Martin, of Friern Park, N12, writes:

George Orwell's visions of Thought Police in *1984* and the writing on the wall in *Animal Farm* are being realized in twenty-first Century Barnet.

The concept of councillors and Town Hall employees as being public servants, for many of the current generation of councillors, has been replaced by their acting and, indeed, imagining themselves to be not servants at all but masters.

This arrogance of power has extended itself to a flawed understanding of such words and concepts as consultation, democracy and now, even cost effectiveness.

Formerly the firm priorities of local government were, firstly, quality of service and, secondly, cost effectiveness.

The relegation to the former of being of minor importance

> **❝** Formerly the priorities of our local governments were, firstly, the quality of service, and, secondly, cost effectiveness.
>
> **Keith Martin**

in the council budget has been accompanied by the extension of so-called cost effectiveness to include such routine gross extravagances as:

■ The employment of overpaid consultants instead of more competent, experienced and less expensive council officers;

■ The unbelievably blind risks inherent in outsourcing public services for 10 or 15 years to

suspect big businesses;

■ The recent totally wasteful fiascos of having an interim library at artsdepot just 200 yards from North Finchley library, as well as the stubborn refusal of a simple dialogue with concerned residents to discuss the reopening of Friern Barnet library.

Instead, they favoured the extravagance and time-wasting of taking the eviction to the County Court of the squatters who, in happy liaison with the community, have for three months provided a shining example to the borough of how a library can and should be run.

This included the sell-out reading and discussion by local celebrity author Will Self of his new novel *Umbrella*, set in Friern Barnet Hospital.

Our elected representatives should study history and learn from their mistakes, not just repeat them.

7

National

Protest squatters celebrate as library tale gets happy ending

Alison Flood

Squatters who have occupied Friern Barnet library in north London for the last five months claimed victory yesterday and said they would move out after the council agreed to hand the library over to the community.

The library was closed by Barnet council last April. The squatters entered the building through an open window in September, restocking shelves with donated books and acting as librarians with the backing of local residents.

In December a judge recognised their right to protest but ruled they could be evicted. But now, following meetings between both sides, an agreement has been reached for the library to be run as a community facility by residents.

"With the council's One Barnet change programme making greater savings than initially predicted, I am pleased that we no longer need to sell this building," said the council leader, Richard Cornelius.

"I've met the trustees of the community library, who are a very committed group of local residents, and I'm looking forward to seeing the new community facility up and running.

The council has given library trustees a licence to be in the library legally for the next month after the squatters move out.

It will award them a two-year lease to run the library, as well as a grant of £25,000 and what Cornelius described as "other practical help".

"There are a lot of very happy people here today," said the activist and squatter Pete Phoenix, a member of the Occupy movement. He was speaking at a ceremony yesterday where the library was handed over by the squatters to the trustees of the newly formed Friern Barnet community library. "It's been five months of direct action and local co-operation [and] we're very happy with a major victory."

Phoenix said residents had been campaigning to save the library for two years, but "as one of the locals said, they'd nearly

Volunteers sort books after the library was occupied and reopened last year

given up hope. They had tried all avenues and were on the point of feeling 'that's it'. Then the building got reoccupied."

"This is a triumph for the local community," said one of the library trustees.

"Our library was closed last April and we were told the building would be marketed. Now we have our library back, with council financial support. We achieved this through constant campaigning, lobbying, and building a broad alliance including squatters, activists, supporters of the Occupy movement, local residents and library campaign groups."

The trustees are seeking 50 volunteers to help run the library, and will continue to push the council for a paid librarian.

The rise of the guerilla library

▶ JOY Locals at saved library yesterday. Above, our story in November.

The People's Library

FRIERN BARNET COMMUNITY LIBRARY REOPENED FEBRUARY 2013

BOOK STOPS HERE..

Locals win battle to run UK's first people's library

EXCLUSIVE

ROS WYNNE-JONES
mirrornews@mirror.co.uk

CAMPAIGNERS who occupied a library closed because of Tory cuts won their battle to have it officially re-opened yesterday

Locals were handed the keys five months after protesters moved in to keep its services alive, making it Britain's first people's library.

The building was shut by council chiefs in April but campaign group Occupy moved in last September.

Now, after months of legal wrangling, the council in Barnet, North London, has caved in and given Friern Barnet Community Library Ltd a temporary lease to keep it open.

Occupy's Pete Phoenix said: "This is a tremendous day."

Maureen Ivens, co-ordinator of the Save Friern Barnet Library Campaign, added: "It's actually better than it was before it was closed.

"The council were only spending a tiny part of their budget on it and it was

getting run down. As a result, fewer people were using it. Now it's become a community hub again." One mum was in tears as the keys were handed over.

She said: "When this library closed, it just was another kick in the teeth."

In November, the Mirror told how residents, activists and writers had kept the library running after it was axed.

Well-wishers donated more than 100,000 books and volunteers refurbished the building, installing second-hand computers and replacing furniture.

The protesters had been given until yesterday to get out after council chiefs won a possession order in December.

But officials relented when they came up with the official body, made up of residents, professionals and librarians.

Occupy said it has invites from across country to reopen closed public spaces.

Mr Phoenix said: "What is happening with libraries is a national disgrace. They are closing or downgrading 317."

There are signs the Government plans to face down occupiers, with an Early Day Motion on squatting public spaces proposed by Tory MP Mike Waverley.

▲ SUCCESS Maureen Ivens in library

9 February 2013   Sky News

London Library reopens despite funding cuts

A north London library reopens to the relief of the local community, but dozens across the nation shut down amid funding cuts.

Campaigners in Friern Barnet have fought to keep their library open. Local rabbi Jeffrey Newman joined the campaign. He said: 'There was a real outburst, there was a real outcry. People felt that something they'd just taken for granted and that they cared about had just been taken away.'

This week Barnet Council agreed various community organisations could take over the premises for the next two years.

Pat Caplan, one of the library's trustees, said: 'I think it shows if you're really determined enough you can make a difference, you can win a little battle even if you can't win the war, and try to do something about preserving a public asset.'

PUBLIC SERVICES

The library that came back from the dead

Author ALAN GIBBONS reports on how Barnet residents have struck a major blow to save their local library from the Tory axe

O NE of the most crushing and demoralising pieces of propaganda spread by governments trying to disarm any opposition is the notion that there is no alternative.

Cuts and austerity are nasty medicine, but you've just got to grimace and swallow.

Last week a unique and effective coalition of local residents, squatters, supporters of the Occupy movement and campaigners won a famous victory.

Five months after occupying Friern Barnet Library, they got Barnet Council to agree to its reopening on a two-year lease. There will be some funding for its running.

That this U-turn about closing a much-loved branch library occurred in Barnet is significant.

The Conservative council has a reputation for widescale outsourcing, an ultra-Tory project.

The idea that there is nothing communities can do to save their local services has taken a palpable hit.

One local activist Mike Gee says of the Conservative council's actions: "I do not fully understand this volte-face but on the face of it, it's wonderful.

"However, we must not forget, this protest is not just about Friern Barnet, one library, it is also about the creeping move to a totalitarian state, the irrational, unjust and draconian cuts to vital public services and job losses that are undermining the very way we live, think and breathe. The antidote is to wake up, open our minds, eyes and hearts and pledge continuing involvement and support to the Occupy movement. Solidarity!"

I spoke to Martin Russo of the Save Friern Barnet Library Group about the implications of this victory in north London.

He tells me how it was achieved: "I think a lot of it is about connecting people, listening to people. The residents care about a public space that serves the community, that is full of children, elderly people coming in for a chat, people doing work experience and using it for education. People are passionate about the building and what it provides."

But how did the campaigners keep going for five long months? Wasn't it a huge drain on their lives?

"We held lots of events. It took a lot of energy to maintain the campaign. The more people you have involved, the easier it is to manage.

"We had a programme of positive events demonstrating why the library was needed. We had people making cakes, events, games for the children.

"We bridged any possible gap between the Occupy group and the residents. The Occupy group gave us the precious resource of time."

A number of commentators have questioned the significance of Friern Barnet's victory.

After all, what has emerged is not a council-run library, but a community resource. At the moment there isn't secure, long-term funding for a full-time librarian.

I was asked during an interview on ITV News last week whether it might not be a pyrrhic victory, more compatible with David Cameron's Big Society than the model of municipal socialism.

Russo disagrees with that point of view. A library that had been closed has risen from the ashes thanks to a popular campaign. But couldn't it be argued that the outcome compromised the idea of libraries as a public service?

"The original campaign was for a publicly run library. To this day, there is strong sentiment in favour of a library service funded by the council with a paid librarian.

"The principle should be that we maintain a public library with a full-time librarian. It is a professional job involving a wide range of skills. Volunteers should complement the job of a librarian, not replace it."

Housing and squatting activist Phoenix agrees.

"We want to make it clear that the activists support the National Libraries Campaign and that putting in place a paid librarian is a priority. I believe consensus has been reached with the community on this point.

"As it stands, the funding offered by the council does not cover a full-time librarian, but as the two-year lease is negotiated and plans go forward, this will be kept at the front of the conversation.

"The activists would like to say that we are strongly opposed to austerity and all the cuts, especially to the library service. We are also strongly opposed to criminalising the homeless and squatters.

"The extreme right of the Conservative Party is seeking to make squatting non-residential buildings also illegal.

"This, if it was successful, would affect all our rights to protest by occupying/squatting space, and would make successful community squat occupations such as the library campaign illegal, thus further removing our rights to shelter and protest."

The Friern Barnet victory is the most positive development in the battle to preserve the public library service since the Charteris report which prevented the closure of 11 Wirral libraries.

Though the outcome fell short of the aim of preserving a council-run service, the community has succeeded in maintaining a valuable resource.

What's more, they generated a remarkable unity between the different strands of the campaign and refused to compromise on the principle of a publicly funded library service with a full-time librarian.

The winds of austerity are not abating. They are gathering force. Eighty per cent of the cuts are still to come.

In Newcastle and my home city of Liverpool 60 per cent of branch libraries are under threat. Winning any kind of victory will be difficult, but Friern Barnet tells us it is not impossible.

Alan Gibbons is a full-time writer, organiser of the Campaign for the Book and a member of the Speak Up for Libraries coalition. His new novel Raining Fire is published by Orion on March 7.

Dates to remember in battle to bring the council to book

Keith Martin of Friern Park, Friern Barnet, writes:

The symmetry of the dates of the Friern Barnet library closure and reopening is clearly coincidental, but the historical significance is enormous.

On Maunday Thursday, April 5, Barnet Council flouted the wishes of the local community by summarily closing the library. Local activists demonstrated their dissent with a six-hour sit-in.

Five months to the day after this, on September 5, squatters entered freely through an open window and reopened the library. Their invitation to the public to come in and donate books and time on the issue desk rota filled the empty shelves to overflowing with 10,000 books, and the rota enabled the library to open six days a week from 10am until 7pm.

The council response was to break off negotiations despite a clear request by the County Court judge to do so, and it took a trial and a second judge's recommendation for negotiation before, five months after the entry, on February 5, 2013, the keys were handed to Friern Barnet Community Library Ltd with a licence to run the library.

Two happy results of the past ten months are that the local community has come together with the squatters to achieve a common aim of restoring the building to be a community library and social centre, and that their determination has succeeded in reversing the actions of the council.

The intention is to employ a full time professional co-ordinator/librarian to lead and tutor a team of volunteer librarians, to man the issue desk, organise events, and raise funds.

The past five months have witnessed the receipt of 10,000 donated books, a full house for the talk by Will Self, and a celebratory lunch on Christmas Day. Now to plan for the next 50 years!

HAM & HIGH   FEB 14 2013

Well done, Friern Barnet!

By Daphne Chamberlain

Friern Barnet has finally regained the library closed by Barnet Council last April. Their victory was achieved through lobbying, protests, attempted negotiations, enormous public support, and dramatic intervention by squatters from the Occupy movement, who have run a service with donated stock since September.

Barnet has now licensed trustees from the local community to use the building until March, when they have been promised a two-year lease, a grant of £25,000 and "other practical help". At last, Friern Barnet have the community library they were refused when Hampstead Garden Suburb was granted one. The next step is to find at least 50 volunteers, and to lobby the Council for a paid librarian.

Polly Napper, from the East Finchley Library Users Group, told *THE ARCHER*: "It is fantastic news that the council is going to allow Friern Barnet library to remain open. I really hope Barnet will follow this excellent decision with an even better one, by employing full time librarians to staff the library again."

OPINION

Heritage Lottery
Library faces stealth cuts

■ **Campaigners who fought to save Friern Barnet Library**

Keith Martin, of Friern Barnet, N12, writes:

RE: (*House is given lottery boost*, H&H, March 7). A tale of two borough councils. The contrast between Camden and Barnet is pronounced. Camden has got it right and Barnet sadly has got it wrong again.

Lauderdale House has been granted a 25-year-lease by Camden, plus a grant of £350,000 and council support for an application to the Heritage Lottery Fund for £800,000.

"We appreciate all the hard work and support from Camden Council to give us the best chance of succeeding with the Heritage Lottery Fund," says Katherine Ives.

Barnet, reliant on the success of the reopened Friern Barnet Community Library for compliance with The Libraries Act 1964, has offered the trustees a two-year lease which denies the library access to Heritage Lottery Fund grants. It is called cuts by stealth. Putting the community first, certainly not.

---

14 March 2013

Barnet Times

Council cutting vital positions

Councillor Richard Cornelius, the Leader of Barnet Borough Council, congratulates himself on the council's 'triumph' of maintaining the same level of council tax by 'dramatically reducing the number of bureaucrats in the town hall.'

Yes, he and his colleagues have systematically deprived the cabinet of the advice of the borough architect, the borough librarian, and the borough arts officer and have outsourced the legal department to Harrow. This policy is called throwing the baby out with the bathwater.

Does the council compensate by inviting stalwarts of the arts scene in the borough to advise it on how to run arts festivals and carnivals? It does not. Instead it employs overpaid consultants who often have little local knowledge, to close a museum and to offer Friern Barnet Community Library a two-year lease, which would deny it access to Heritage Lottery Fund grants. It is called cuts by stealth. Putting the community first it is not.

Keith Martin

Friern Park
Friern Barnet

ANALYSIS | Heritage boost

Lauderdale revamp is given lottery windfall

Plans for historic house a step closer due to £800,000 grant

by Emma Youle
emma.youle@archant.co.uk

A treasured historic house in Highgate has won a lottery grant of £800,000 to transform parts of the Grade II listed property and secure its long term financial future.

Staff and volunteers at Lauderdale House, in Waterlow Park, are celebrating after winning the Heritage Lottery Fund grant, which was announced on Tuesday.

Sue Bowers, head of the Heritage Lottery Fund for London, said: "Lauderdale House is now well on its way to being transformed and we are delighted to support this project.

"As a rare survivor with Tudor origins the house is of national importance and well loved by the community. Once works are complete they'll be able enjoy it once more and for future generations."

Lauderdale House Society, which runs the house, is now two thirds of the way towards raising the £1.8million it needs to embark on its ambitious Lauderdale Transformed project.

Community help

The major redevelopment will overhaul run-down areas of the house to create modern facilities – including a state-of-the-art glass-fronted workshop with views across Waterlow Park.

Camden Council has given £350,000 and along with a grant of £48,000 from BIFFA Award and other fundraising of £15,000, the fundraising tally stands at just over £1.2million.

But community help is needed to reach the final hurdle and get

■ Katherine Ives celebrates with staff, volunteers and board members
Picture: Nigel Sutton

the £1.8million so work can begin.

Director Katherine Ives said: "We're not there yet. We still need another £600,000 before we can start the work. This seems daunting, but just over a year ago we had just under £10,000 for the project and are now two thirds of the way to success.

"We are applying to trusts and foundations but we also need the support of our local community to make this happen.

"Every donation will help us, whether it's a cheque with several noughts or the contents of someone's penny jar.

"This is a once-in-a-lifetime opportunity to "transform" our historic house and programme, ensuring our future and transforming the experience of every visitor."

The Heritage Lottery Fund grant is the culmination of more than

five years of hard work by staff and volunteers.

Some 1,500 hours of volunteer time have so far been spent to transform the Grade II listed house, which has been a landmark on Highgate's skyline since Elizabethan times and is now a thriving arts and education centre welcoming thousands of visitors a year.

Nick Peacey, chairman of Lauderdale House, said: "This is the opportunity to complete the total transformation we have worked for since I became involved with Lauderdale House when it was a burnt out shell 35 years ago.

"It can guarantee the house's future as a resource for the community and preserve and celebrate the history of this unique building."

For more information on the project or to donate, visit www.lauderdalehouse.co.uk

APRIL 18 2013

THE PRESS

COMMENT

Library needs to be given more funding

WHILE it was a major victory for the squatters and residents who ran a successful campaign to keep Friern Barnet Library open, serious challenges lie ahead.

The council has committed a mere £25,000 a year to the facility – and it is hard to see how this will be enough to run the library for 12 months.

For instance, there is. very little funding to improve the building, which has been left in disrepair, and there is no money to employ any staff.

Is this meant to be an example of David Cameron's Big Society?

The community group running the building is serious about turning the space into more than just a library, with music nights, discussion evenings and film nights planned.

Councillors should realise sooner rather than later that this is an invaluable community asset which should receive an appropriate level of funding in order to function properly.

Listen to the judge's advice

The report of Maria Nash's High Court action ('No end to battle', *Times Series,* May 2) ends by quoting the Barnet Borough Council leader Richard Cornelius, who suggests that her appeal would incur 'even more costs that will have to be met from public funds'.

It is surprising and disappointing to read such irresponsible views put forward by a man in his position. He seems totally cocooned from reality, surrounded as he is by Philistine acolytes on his cabinet.

A judicial review is about justice. Can the council legitimately ignore the view of the judge that but for a technicality – the paperwork was not submitted in time – he would have ruled in favour of Ms Nash?

For Councillor Cornelius to claim otherwise is misguided. His assertion that further public funds will have to be spent is untrue and wasteful in the extreme. To jettison the One Barnet programme would at a stroke remove the risky and stupid gamble which it represents, and cease the waste of precious funds that should be used to enable groups such as Age UK Barnet to provide the care for elderly and vulnerable people, which they were doing before the council cut their grant.

Above all, the council should accept the advice of the judge and not sign these major outsourcing contracts because it is morally wrong to do so. It is no part of the job of our elected representatives to victimise disabled pensioners or needlessly make 400 council staff redundant and unemployed.

Keith Martin

Friern Park
Friern Barnet

THE PRESS
COMMENT

Stepping down: Andrew Harper has quit as a member of the council's cabinet

THE announcement that Andrew Harper has relinquished his position as cabinet member for youth services (*The Press*, May 23) is a sore loss to the council.

Even worse is the news the rest of the cabinet remains unchanged.

An opportunity exists to strengthen the portfolio for arts and libraries, where Robert Rams has shown a consistent antagonism to culture in

Barnet, closing a museum and a library and culminating in torpedoing his own library strategy by pulling out of the planned landmark library at artsdepot.

There are several Conservative councillors with a sympathy for the arts. For example, David Longstaff, also in the cabinet, is chairman of Incognito Theatre and on the town team board, designated with the

Open up the cabinet to arts-friendly councillors

regeneration of Tally Ho.

The arts in Barnet are well served by Barnet Borough Arts Council, which is no part of the council.

The artists, musicians, writers and people of the area deserve a cabinet member in sympathy with what is being achieved, despite council apathy.

Keith Martin

Friern Park, Friern Barnet

One Barnet continues to polarise opinions

I AM afraid that I have been moved to write by the inaccuracy of your recent editorial (*The Press*, May 30).

There should be at least a cursory effort to understand the actual situation, both in terms of outsourcing and Your Choice.

There is no "relentless drive to outsource all service provision". Instead, each service area has been looked at and the best method of delivery identified.

We are bringing recycling back in-house, sharing public health and legal services with Harrow, embarking on a joint-venture project and, yes, outsourcing some back-office functions.

These changes will protect and improve service quality and in no way represent a "race to the bottom".

We have also established a trading company, The Barnet Group, of which Your Choice is a subsidiary.

The reason for this set-up is entirely logical: the increased usage of direct payments means that many people are barred from purchasing services direct from the council.

Without placing council services with an arm's-length provider, excellent services such as the Rosa Morison day centre could not be accessed and used by the majority.

Your Choice is designed to create a service people can and will choose, balancing quality and cost.

Reporters have a duty to challenge and be sceptical about the council,

Hitting back: Richard Cornelius

but should apply this equally to those who criticise us.

I wonder, for example, if the Tirza Waisel quoted of CADDSS is one and the same with the synonymous BAPS coordinator and whether this relationship is representative of that between the organisations?

A hard-left pressure group should be subject to as much scrutiny as anyone else.

Councillor Richard Cornelius
Leader of Barnet Council

❑ RICHARD Cornelius claims

("The wait must go on", *The Press*, June 6) that "the cost of delaying the outsourcing contracts could be more than £700,000 per month".

I ask him:

● Why the council did not agree to hold the judicial review on the July date booked by the court?

● If the delay was caused by council staff double-booking their barrister, why did they not save expense by appointing someone available?

● If the delay was influenced by outsourcing Barnet legal services to Harrow Council, can efficiency be resumed by taking it back in-house?

● Have you reconsidered the alternative of deciding now to cut your losses and cancel the hugely risky plans for outsourcing public services?

It may well be the most sensible and cost-effective solution to the whole problem, especially if accompanied by a proper reconsideration of the alternative plans put forward by Unison for in-house solutions.

The employment of council staff within the borough will further stimulate the local economy where businesses are struggling and need encouragement.

Keith Martin
Friern Park,
Friern Barnet

❑ Since this letter was received, the hearing has been brought forward to July 15-16

CHAPTER 3

Every Wednesday evening, upstairs at the Royal British Legion on the corner of Ramsden Road, next to the green outside Friern Barnet library, the conspirators of Save Friern Barnet Library Group (SFBLG) met to plot how the library might be reopened.

They assembled evidence to present to Barnet Council of the astonishing surge of public support for it to reopen. And it was astonishing. People donated books for a Saturday People's Library on the green; one supporter painted a new sign:

Others donated gazebos for shelter in the event of rain (this was April in England, remember), and the book stock needed to be protected.

So on 14 April, nine days after the summary closure of the library, a sunny day and pink cherry blossom welcomed the first of many regular Saturday appearances of the Pop-up Library. The books were laid out on trestle tables, divided into Fiction, Children's books, Non-Fiction, Sport and Cookery.

And there were cakes and drinks. Lots of people came and there was a cheerful party atmosphere to the proceedings.

This became a regular Saturday event. A professional touch was the printing and glueing inside the book covers of a label, proclaiming that

This book is the property of Friern Barnet People's Library.

The variety of expertise and enthusiasm among the community was manifest. As was the organization of the Save Friern Barnet Library Group. Under the capable chairmanship of, in succession:

> Fiona Cochrane,
> Martin Russo, who brought communication skills and
> contacts within BBC Radio and TV,
> and Maureen Ivens,

the committee organized the Saturday pop-up libraries on the green, applications for the status of the library as a listed building and the adjacent green as a Village Green.

Also the enthusiasm of parents of young children such as Fiona Cochrane and Tamar Andrusier reinforced the contacts with local schools and brought the welcome participation of schoolchildren in the Saturday Libraries on the Green.

The media coverage began with the bloggers and local press, and soon spread to press interviews and features in documentary films.

A film crew from the BBC The One Show came to film the Pop-up Library, and the feature on prime time national television on 22 May 2012 included an interview with Melvyn Bragg, who described the importance to him as a schoolboy of his local library. The BBC do this sort of thing very well, and their detailed coverage contrasted the experience of two local communities who had each harnessed volunteers to provide a library service. The predominantly well-off residents of Chalfont-St-Giles in nearby Buckinghamshire, who had presented to their local council a plan for a reopened library to be manned completely by volunteers; and Friern Barnet, where the aim of the SFBLG, as clearly described on the programme by their Chair Martin Russo, was to support the national library profession by engaging a professional librarian to encourage, teach and support the volunteers. Martin was shown first at Friern Barnet Library, then at Chalfont-St-Giles, where he was taken by the reporter to see the set-up and talk to the people running the Community Library there. Martin's reaction was that he felt it could not work in the same way at Friern Barnet.

Other landmarks that summer were that more people with cameras came to interview anyone willing to talk. The interviewers ranged from local schoolchildren to correspondents from Australia and Japan. And they all enjoyed featuring the Saturday library on the green.

One of the film crews was the American singer Charlie Honderich, who shot the fifteen-minute documentary film *A Tale of Two Barnets,* produced by Roger Tichborne. The film begins with a powerful interview with the film director Ken Loach, whose own feature-length documentary *Spirt of '45* has been acclaimed in 2013. *A Tale of Two Barnets* was premiered on 19 March 2012 at The Phoenix East Finchley to a capacity audience of about 300 people.

The sequel *Barnet: the billion pound Gamble* had its premiere too at The Phoenix on 22 October 2012. In it many of the same interviewees brought the viewing public up-to-date with their stories seven months on.

Other excuses for celebration on a Saturday morning on the green were on 3 June 2012, when the occasion of Queen Elizabeth II nd's Jubilee was graced with a visit from Cllr Kate Salinger, Deputy Mayor of Barnet, in an enormous pink hat, with her husband Cllr Brian Salinger. Kate remained a consistently a staunch supporter of the library in her own Coppetts Ward, in marked contrast to almost all other Conservative councillors, who stayed in the camp of the totally Philistine Cllr Robert Rams who, although the Cabinet member with responsibility for culture, took no pleasure whatsoever in what for most people would have been the most enjoyable remit on the Council. Rams not only failed to meet Will Self, the Booker-nominated author, who came to the library on 14 November to speak to a packed audience and read from his novel *Umbrella,* largely set in Friern

ROSIE CANNING AND BIKE

Hospital opposite. He had not met Jacqui Dankworth on her appearance in the London Jazz Festival at artsdepot, nor the actors Timothy West and Prunella Scales when they gave a poetry reading there.

Back to the 3 June Jubilee, others at the library on the green were jazz singer and guitarist Arnie Donoff and the singer Talibah, who provided the entertainment under the cherry tree.

On 21 July there was a demonstration by Barnet Alliance for Public Services, which took the form of a march from the library to Victoria Park in Ballards Lane, Finchley. The themes echoed on placards were opposition to the Council plans for outsourcing in its One Barnet policy, and RE-OPEN FRIERN BARNET LIBRARY NOW !
The route of the march took it past Helen Michael's Café Buzz in North Finchley, the *rive gauche* rendez-vous of activists, bloggers and revolutionaries of the borough.

On 26 August Kim Lee had the inspiration of celebrating the centenary of the 43 bus, which since 1912 had run from its terminus in Friern Barnet Road, via Muswell Hill and Archway to London Bridge Station. The local historian David Berguer provided archive photos of the bus from earlier epochs. Open air double deckers, single deckers coach-style.

Thus the movement gathered strength. But the Council remained unmoved. UNTIL SEPTEMBER 5th.

GEOFF AND JANET LEIFER

MARYLA PERSAK-ENEFER AND ROGER TICHBORNE

MARYLA PERSAK-ENEFER AT THE DOOR

BARRY, ROGER, BARBARA AND BOB

CHERRY BLOSSOM

QUEEN'S JUBILEE – CLLR KATE SALINGER

ARNIE DONOFF AND TALIBAH

news in brief

Interim library opens in North Finchley

Barnet Council's new interim library service in North Finchley has opened its doors to residents.

Based in the artsdepot building at Tally Ho Corner, the library opened on 24 April and offers a collection of around 10,000 items of stock as well as newspapers and magazines. There are study tables, comfortable seating and a children's area.

Plans are also being made for a reading group, reading scheme for under-fives and for links with nearby schools.

The interim service has been set up while plans are developed for a permanent Landmark Library within artsdepot.

The interim library's opening hours are:
Tuesdays 2pm – 5pm, Wednesdays and Thursdays 10am – 1pm and Fridays 2pm – 5pm.

For more information on the library service visit www.barnet.gov.uk/libraries

Re-open Friern Barnet Library Group

We aim to re-open the library 3-4 days a week – 11am-3pm

This is your community library, come in, say hello, sign up for the rota.

We need books, librarians, donations, tables, chairs, videos and food. We are planning workshops, skill shares and film showings.

Please come and help re-open the library – an action is worth a thousand words.
Caretakers phone: 07592 231150

Re-open Friern Barnet Library Group

HELEN MICHAEL AT CAFÉ BUZZ

CHAPTER 4

SEPTEMBER 2012 TO JANUARY 2013   THE SQUATTERS

Mike Freer, MP for Finchley and Golders Green, was instrumental in promoting legislation passed by Parliament making it unlawful for squatters to occupy residential property. He had been active especially on behalf of constituents in Hampstead whose empty second homes were thus occupied.

The immediate effect of this legislation was an activity on the grapevine of homeless squatters, who were obliged suddenly to seek other buildings in which to sleep. Thus it was that a message emanated from Occupy, the centre of information for the tents of squatters on the steps of St Paul's Cathedral the previous December, that a window of the closed Friern Barnet Library would be open on 5 September. The source of this information was a secret.

The Occupy movement, far from its depiction by such as the Daily Mail as consisting of irresponsible scroungers without respect for property, was able to hand pick a small group of squatters from Camden Town with, among their number, a former librarian, and all of them young and enthusiastic, to invite the community to donate books and time to join them in reopening the library.

Despite the initial hesitancy of some of the SFBLG committee to 'trespass' and thus break the law, there was an instant and infectious welcome from other activists. Notably Rosie Canning, a creative writer and co-founder with Lindsay Bamfield of Greenacre Writers, who had instituted a petition to the Council to reopen the library, has said how she was excited at the prospect of this unexpected turn of events. So too was Mike Gee, Environment spokesman for the Finchley Society and a skilled carpenter.

The principal reason for the swift acceptance of the squatters and their plans was without doubt the ability, enthusiasm, experience and personality of their leader, Phoenix. He is totally at ease in dealing with people both in authority and of the community. He it was who, in liaison with the leaders of the local community, planned how to man the issue desk, and organised four what I call Think Tanks with representatives of Barnet Council. In these he demonstrated his skills of negotiation with the town hall team, and ability to run a fluent and productive meeting. He acted as facilitator (chair) and patiently but effectively got matters aired and decisions taken. This was so effective that after four such meetings the Council, who had not once sent one of their elected representatives but were represented by town hall staff with no power to take decisions – just to report back for action by the councillors - decided summarily to cancel the fifth Think Tank and instead to institute proceedings for the eviction of the occupants, before the negotiations would have the chance to lead to an inevitable reopening of the library.

One example of Phoenix's skills was his ability at a meeting to harness and channel the passion of Mike Gee, a skill beyond the ability of Councillor Hugh Rayner, Chair at a Council Scrutiny Committee!

A flavour of this is contained in this extract from Rosie Canning's masterly minutes of the first Think Tank at the library on 10 September, (just five days after the occupation!):

> Heather Wills (Council) – Capital receipt from sale of FBL might be £430,000. Part of the library strategy for improving literacy.

> Mike Gee – You closed this library to improve literacy! Excuse me while I fall on the floor.

Here are the full minutes of that meeting:

<u>Re-open Friern Barnet Library Group</u>

Minutes of meeting held September 10th 2012 10am between local residents and London Borough of Barnet.
Friern Barnet Library, Friern Barnet Road, London N11 3DS

Present: Pete Phoenix – Facilitator (PP), Mike Gee (MG), Rosie Canning (RC), Julie Taylor (JT), Mike Fahey (MF), Heather Wills (HW), Craig Cooper (CC), Paul – Local Resident (P), Keith Martin (KM), John Dix (JD), Diane Taylor (DT), Fiona Brickwood (FB), Ollie Natelson (ON), David Cope (DC), Julia Hines (JH), Kirsty – Local resident (K), Maella – Local resident (M), Ann Levens (AL), Roger Tichbourne (RT), Theresa Musgrove (TM), Pauline Coakley-Webb (PC-W), Daniel (D), Petra (P), Daniel Cope (DC), Arjun Mittra (AM)
Minutes written by: Rosie Canning

Introductions: Everyone introduced themselves
PP – We're looking for solutions and dialogue – appreciate LBB budget situation – how do we all cooperate to make this work? Residents of Friern Barnet would like FBL to stay open, we're also looking at Friary House – in FBL during interim period.
JT – Process point – Cllr. Robert Rams is on honeymoon.
RT – Couldn't some other councillor attend, for example Cornelius?
JT – Richard Cornelius, will be happy to get involved in Cllr Rams's absence.

PP – Asked council to send via email, some models for running libraries e.g. Hampstead Garden Suburb (HGS).

JT – LBB have supported HGS and offered visit to library. Low cost solution, keen to see a community library in this library. From LBB point of view use this synergy to make something happen.

MG – Pointed out there could be no compromise over relocation – would be like taking the heart out of the community – this library purpose-built, therefore it might be hard to compromise.

TM – Why has it taken the occupation the occupation for LBB to start negotiations? Doesn't it set a precedent for squatters? Phoenix has managed to achieve what the local community could not.

JT – There have been a large number of meetings about Friary Park House.

JH - Disabled access – no vehicle access – how will this be dealt with? Explained about problems with Friary House.

AM – LBB subsidised HGS, feasible here, would LBB be prepared to subsidise a library here?

JT – Financial difference – LBB don't own the building, we are tied into a lease. FBL – we own the freehold and can sell this building. Keen to make a success of Friary Park, good to have a hub/library there.

MG – In 2012/13, council say they saved £110,000 per year saved by closing FBL not true cost due to costs of running artsdepot £34,200 in rent alone, as well as closing down costs of FBL, librarian at artsdepot – LBB have not saved £110,000 per year.

PP – Asked LBB for a copy of the accounts.

HW – Absolutely.

AM – Is it meeting room one in Friary House that LBB are making available?

HW – Meeting room one is the largest.

AM – Management of Friary House is bad – Refugee Service moved out because of this.

KM – FBL is purpose built and could be opened tomorrow. Friary House not a library. Something like £40 per book to run artsdepot – costly mistake, costs could be saved by closing artsdepot tomorrow. Why should residents money be spent on this?

ON – How does floor area of Friary House compare to FBL? Land next to FBL could be sold and money made from sale/rent of properties.

FB –Building flats will destroy FB community. Library was the community. LBB had no remit to go ahead with closure of FBL and plans for artsdepot room – the library strategy clearly demonstrated that 73% of residents did not agree with artsdepot proposal – therefore the council had no remit to pursue this. Carnegie Trust built FBL for as long as the community want it, in perpetuity. Was this put on the deeds? Has desire to get people into work, hub working towards this, community support for this.

JT – LBB remit is to support people back to work, support literacy, support community. How can we make Friary House attractive?

M – What about saving this building which is accessible for people with physical disabilities and is also in walking distance for people with other disabilities.

RC – If 73% of residents don't want a library at artsdepot then why close North Finchley, keep it open, re-open FBL as an interim measure. How much money would be saved by this measure?

RT – Older people use libraries to save on their heating bills, they use libraries to stay alive. FBL within walking distance for people with toddlers. If LBB did not sell FBL, the council would not grind to a halt, they would survive.

JT – Accept we don't have complete handle on who uses the library – might be better answer to deal with the problems.

RC – Libraries were built to serve the local community. According to 1931 Census, population of Friern Barnet was 23,101. Population has doubled (around 41,000) so there should be more libraries and not less.

MG – Have you been approached by any developer? Does the sale include any land? Will the library be demolished? How long will it take to sell the library?

CC – Not in discussion with any developer. We intend to sell the library and land to the side, depending on the pending village green application. Whether it will be developed or knocked down will be up to the developer. 6months – 18months. It hasn't been marketed yet. People know it is available.

PC-W – Parking easy outside FBL. Where will people park outside Friary House? Sticking point – The council representatives here today don't have the authority to talk about this library. Consider adding surgery costs, £60 per hour to the cost of closing FBL.

FB – When Cllr Rams put sale of FBL through last year, he made an error – sale of the building goes into the property budget.

JT – Capital budget for libraries – invest capital to save revenue, this is how it works.

FB – Closed library building, Rams is out. Which councillor is dealing with this now?

JT – Councillor Thomas

RT – Cllr Thomas and Cllr Rams should be at the next meeting.

P – Safety issues – children, single women, older people, walking through the park to Friary House in the dark.

PP – We need subsequent meetings to discuss these issues.

HW – Capital receipt of FBL £430,000. Council's decision not Ram's. Part of the library strategy for improving literacy.

MG – You closed this library to improve literacy! Excuse me while I fall on the floor.

DT – Is LBB intending implementing eviction procedures? Is LBB striking a caretaker agreement?

JT – Not making any snap decisions on that.

M- FBL is under review for heritage status, how will this effect the sale of the building?

CC – Any developer would have to take listing into account.

JD – This meeting is futile, lovely chat but the council representatives here are not authorised to discuss this building. We need a meeting with those that are authorised to talk about FBL and get this on the agenda.

PP – Asked about different library models.

HW – Surrey, Bucks and Lewisham, many different models - degree of support varies. We've learnt a lot with HGS.

MF – HGS building not property of council. Lease that stipulates the building must be used as a public library. HGS have their own library management system, book stock was passed to the community library with a supply of new books give, plus access to our books lending scheme.

PP – More information is needed from other libraries, SFBL don't want a voluntary library, we need people to fill in the rota to keep it running. Cooperative negotiation – continue this process. Working solution for this building for six months to a year.

PP- Thanked everyone for attending.

The Council, wrong-footed by Phoenix in the Think Tanks, did no better in the eviction proceedings. At the first, at St Mary's Crown Court, Finchley Central on 18 September, the judge recommended that both sides meet to negotiate a mutually satisfactory resolution of the library occupation.

BBC 1 TV London News on 13 September aired interviews at both 1.30 pm and different ones at 6.30 pm.
Phoenix concentrated on the negotiations with the Council to try to find a solution for the library and the Council's emphasis on it moving elsewhere, such as Friary House in the secluded Friary Park. Statements by other library users – women with small children and refugee families grateful for its existence – were contrasted with an interview with the Council Leader Richard Cornelius.

At the second hearing on 10 October a new judge set out a timetable to allow for negotiation, then mediation if necessary and finally, if this failed to achieve a satisfactory solution, trial – the most expensive option – on 17 and 18 December. Thus a further two months grace.

The Council reaction was not to negotiate at all but to choose by far the most expensive option and go to trial.

BBC 1 TV Sunday Politics at 11 am on 2 December 2012 concentrated for nine minutes on Barnet Council's outsourcing proposals, described by its opponents as an enormous billion-pound gamble. The footage then cut to Friern Barnet Library, showing the

Occupy Revolution banner and Phoenix, captioned as a Community Campaigner, talking about the importance of space for people to live in.

CHAPTER 5

31 JULY 2012   ROSIE'S PETITION

It is worth reiterating some of the events surrounding Rosie Canning's petition to the Council for the reopening of the library, and Robert Rams's arrogant and insolent disdain for it.

Because of the size of the petition, Rosie was invited to address the Scrutiny Committee on 31 July 2012, where the Chair Hugh Rayner decided that the petition be referred not, as one would have supposed, to the Cabinet, but to the Cabinet MEMBER responsible, that is, Robert Rams.
So how does he act?
He posts this "Petition update" on the internet, preceding Rosie's petition!
Here it is:

Petition to RE-OPEN FRIERN BARNET LIBRARY

This petition is now closed, as its deadline has passed. (Editor's note: inaccurate!)
We the undersigned petition Barnet Council to RE-OPEN FRIERN BARNET LIBRARY.

Submitted by ROSIE CANNING –
Deadline to sign up by 10 April 2013 (sic)

Petition update from the council, 06 August 2012, while petition was still open

Dear Petitioner,

Thank you for taking the time to sign a petition relating to Friern Barnet library.

No Council takes a decision to close a library lightly – I, like you, value Barnet's libraries very highly and am proud of their vital contribution to literacy among our children.

Unfortunately, the current economic climate means that the Council has to save £46million across 3 years, and the library service has to take its share of this. Unlike some other councils, Barnet Council has chosen to make these savings as part of a clear strategy to improve our library service and make it fit for the future – reinvesting in improved facilities in which we can all be proud, and taking into account the needs of the whole borough.

Our strategy ensured that we are now putting literacy at the heart of everything we do, opening our libraries up for longer and ensuring that every primary school child becomes a library member.

When making this difficult decision, the Council did consider a wide range of options, including the potential to create a community library at Friary House: unfortunately no community group took up this offer or was able to submit a robust business proposal for any other premises.

In response to requests, the Council has opened an interim library at Tally Ho Corner, as we work hard to develop plans for a landmark library at artsdepot.

Although we have been asked to reopen the Friern Barnet library building, no one has come up with a robust alternative to the saving we need to make to meet the budget set for the service by full Council.

As a result, while I have considered the request made in the petition, I am unable to agree to reverse the decision made by the Council's Cabinet in July 2011.

I am sorry that this is disappointing news for you.

Yours sincerely

Cllr Robert Rams
Cabinet Member for Customer Access and Partnerships

More details from petition creator

We the residents, students and workers of Friern Barnet, are petitioning Barnet Council to RE-OPEN our local library. Friern Barnet Library in its present place and shape is an integral part of community life in the surrounding area. We want a cheerful Local library. This is a chance for Barnet Council to show they ARE listening to local residents and reverse the bad feeling caused by the closure of this lovely library.

Blog for the Better Barnet website by Keith Martin

SCRUTINY COMMITTEE 31 July 2012

It was a long agenda.

Hendon Football Club/Jewish School – referred back

Parking

Events in the parks

Old people's centre cuts

Youth centre cuts

Then Rosie Canning's petition to reopen Friern Barnet library. Rosie presented her case calmly and persuasively. The closure decision was taken prematurely. The interim library at artsdepot was an inefficient failure.

Along with other people in the public gallery I had submitted two questions for the Public Questions slot. All of them were ruled inappropriate for the meeting, on the rather curious grounds that they referred to a matter upon which a decision had been taken during the last six months. Never mind that the decision (to close Friern Barnet library) was palpably flawed as made upon false information, but let that pass. One would have thought that questions querying the validity of Council decisions were very much what a Scrutiny Committee would wish to hear.

The validity of excluding the questions was questioned at the meeting with good reason by Cllr Pauline Coakley Webb. She made the unanswerable point that reopening the library, the object of the petition, was clearly a different matter from the cited decision, which was to close it. One-nil to her, but of course it was too late to resurrect the questions and obtain written answers by 9pm in the evening. Cllr Hugh Rayner, the Chair, informed us all that written replies would be communicated to the questioners. Sure enough, I received a reply to my two today. As ever, the answers were evasive and failed to come close to answering the questions. There must be a textbook at the Town Hall in How to give Evasive Answers. For the record:

Q 1   Can you confirm that the interim library at Tally Ho will be closed and replaced by the reopened Friern Barnet library, and give the date when this will happen?

Ball park estimates of the cost per loan of books from the interim library amount to about £40 per book loan, which is clearly a wasteful use of resources and money. Rent of the room at artsdepot is about £30,000 pa, staffing and other costs say £20,000, thus a total of £50,000 pa = about £1,000 per week.

Observation of books borrowed puts it at a maximum of 25 per week, hence the calculation of £40 per loan.

One would presume that sound management would demand a swift end to such unnecessary extravagance, and a very welcome return of the comprehensive and cost effective service offered at Friern Barnet.

Response 1   The libraries strategy is clear that Friern Barnet has been closed to deliver savings and to enable the merger of services into a new landmark library at artsdepot. The Tally Ho Corner library is an interim facility provided in response to demand.
Projecting current performance across the rest of the year, the current cost per issue is £6.03, compared to £2.68 in 2011/12 at Friern Barnet library. The total running costs of the library are £32,400 per annum.

Q 2   Please would you make available for the Scrutiny Committee to read before their deliberations on 31 July, and published for the general public also, the feasibility study for the Landmark Library at artsdepot, so long delayed since July 2011 but promised belatedly by the end of June 2012, together with the brief given to the architect?

Response 2   We are happy to respond to requests for information in line with the Council's governance framework.

Of course my two Supplementary questions never got an airing but, for the benefit of councillors reading this, here they are:

1   IT WOULD SEEM THAT THE DECISION TO PUT AN
INTERIM LIBRARY INTO ARTSDEPOT WAS A COSTLY
FAILURE.

DOES THE CABINET EVER CONSIDER THE CRITERION OF
COST EFFECTIVENESS BEFORE MAKING DECISIONS
INVOLVING LONG TERM CONTRACTS?

2   IN 1999 BARNET'S BOROUGH ARCHITECT, VAUGHAN
ABBOT, VISITED CHAVILLE, ONE OF BARNET'S TWIN
TOWNS, TO STUDY THEIR ARTS CENTRE. THIS WAS IN
THE DAYS WHEN CONSULTATION PROCESSES WERE
TAKEN SERIOUSLY BY THE COUNCIL.

DOES THE CABINET AGREE THAT, WITH
HINDSIGHT, THERE ARE MANY CURRENT
EXAMPLES OF THE BENEFITS TO RESIDENTS TO BE
HAD FROM HAVING ON THE TOWN HALL STAFF A
PROFESSIONALLY QUALIFIED BOROUGH
ARCHITECT?

Next it was Kate Salinger who tore into her Tory colleagues and their stupid decisions. She described her former visits with her children to Friern Barnet library after school and contrasted it with a bus trip in the current century with children from Friern Barnet to Tally Ho. The interim library is a PALTRY SOP, and not a patch on what is offered by North Finchley library round the corner. It is a complete waste of money.

Barry Rawlings was impassioned.

"For God's sake, to close the library during the run-up to school exams...!"

Robert Rams, rather than facing this onslaught chose to put in to bat Bill Murphy, the Assistant Director of Libraries. Unfortunately Bill was as out of his depth as Robert.

"I have to make savings...We need the capital receipt from sale of the libraries..."
Council finance, he explained to us, is complicated. Too much so for him. His simple mantra is based on the faulty premise that there are no other ways to skin a cat. The budget exercise, as he should know, is about whether or not to increase Council tax, whether to use reserves, lots more.
Brian Salinger asked, as he had at the Scrutiny Committee which had recommended that the library remain open (and been met by prevarication and non-information), WHEN was it planned for the Landmark library to open, and where would it be in the building? Cllr Rams's famous hope that "the gap" between closing FBL and opening one at artsdepot would be weeks rather than months, was revised to "2013 or 2014."
Where would it be? What the scrutineers required was an honest answer. Would it be in the two-floor gym, vacant and unoccupied for eight years? Not Robert Rams's vague "Oh, it could be anywhere." This would have been an appropriate moment to tell us what the feasibility study recommends.

The prevarication and misinformation was too much for Mike Gee in the public seats, and he was goaded to interrupt the flow of nonsense. Hugh Rayner, in the Chair, let down by Murphy and Rams, gave Mike an ultimatum to be silent or be ejected. Mike himself felt insulted and deserving an apology, so Hugh adjourned the meeting for a cooling off. A modicum of honest debate and accurate information from Murphy and Rams would have avoided the outburst.

The irony of this is that Mike, who is Environment and Transport representative on the Finchley Society committee, is one of those experienced local residents whose advice the Cabinet so signally lacks, and who should be invited to advise Council committees. Until they begin to heed sound advice they will continue to blunder on to the detriment of the health of the borough.

Keith Martin
1 August 2012

CHAPTER 6

18 SEPTEMBER 2012   CONFLICT OF INTEREST ?

Barnet Council were initially conciliatory in their approach to the squatters in the library, offering them Friary House to accommodate the reopened library instead of Friern Barnet Library. Negotiations to discuss various alternatives to a site for the library and a home for the squatters seemed to be proceeding in an atmosphere of calm. The word 'squatters' was not used, and the term 'occupants' gave an impression of respectability to the group who were in negotiation with the Council.

This calm was then broken by the Council commencing an action for the eviction of the squatters from the library.

The action for eviction was scheduled for a preliminary hearing at the County Court in Finchley on Tuesday 18 September 2012.
The judge at one point called for a short break in the proceedings to allow people to consider whether or not to be co-defendants with the occupants. I had a word with Phoenix and volunteered to be one such. I was aware that it might be a useful contribution, to show the Council and the Court that at least one local resident was on trial.

I was aware too that I had a conflict of interest. As a Council-tax payer,
I was appalled at the Council wasting my money in bringing the action.
As Keith Martin, I would be a co-defendant.

I declare a small conflict of interest.
It's an interesting place to be at.
With one hand I'm assaulting the Council,
With the other evicting the squat.

When I started to try a discussion,
I was clear and direct in my aim.
'Twas to keep Friern library open,
And spare the poor readers the pain.

Oh, Democracy, where are you going?
Will it end with the freedom we crave?
Right to work, right to act, to protest,
Or shiver and die in our grave?

What we share are the rights to our freedom.
When we walk from this Court, we walk tall.
We proclaim, be we rich or impov'rished,
There's no conflict of interest at all.

18 SEPT 2012 CELEBRATIONS AT THE COURT HOUSE

PHOENIX AND TWO PRESS REPORTERS OUTSIDE THE
COURT HOUSE

Film showing
BILLION POUND GAMBLE
Starring Barnet residents and Ken Loach
Monday 22 October, 6pm
Phoenix Cinema, Finchley

Also coming soon:
Public Meeting in November – see local newspaper for details.

If you would like to find out more information please contact Barnet Alliance for Public Services:
Website: http:// barnetalliance.org
Email: barnetalliance4publicservices@gmail.com
Twitter: @BarnetAlliance

OUR BARNET

Barnet Alliance for Public Services
Summer 2012

THE BILLION POUND GAMBLE

CAN THE PEOPLE OF BARNET REALLY AFFORD THE ONE BARNET PROGRAMME?

HYMN HORIZONTAL WITH PLACARDS

labour4barnet.com

Working hard for Finchley and Golders Green

Special Edition

The Local Voice

abour ouncillors orking r you

this edition

hat is the e Barnet ogramme?

orking for e things you re about

ghting for irer parking arges

Barnet Tories' Library policy is in chaos

Labour is opposed to shutting the Friern Barnet Library

North Finchley Library – very little space to expand further

proposed site of 'Landmark' Library – now scrapped

East Finchley Library

Labour speaking up for our local Libraries

Following the announcement by Conservative Cabinet Member Councillor Robert Rams that he has dropped his high profile plan to build a Landmark Library at the artsdepot, Labour's Libraries Spokesperson and Woodhouse Ward Councillor, Anne Hutton said:

'The Tories' Library policy is in complete chaos. They closed Friern

Barnet Library under the pretext of 'merging' it into this Landmark Library at the artsdepot, which has now been abandoned. They have wasted thousands of pounds on a temporary Library at the artsdepot, and on a feasibility study, and although Councillor Rams says he will now invest in North Finchley Library there is very little space to do so because the upper floor is

used as an outreach children's centre. Councillor Rams also states that local people want a Library at Friary House - but nobody knows who he is talking about, because all the Library campaigners I know think this site is completely unsuitable. The whole thing is an absolute omnishambles.'

CHAPTER 7

1 November 2012   Waaaaaaaaaaah! Mr Mustard

I saw some slides from a recent feasibility study dated 3 July 2012 for installing a "Landmark Library" in the artsdepot, a doomed idea which has now been kicked into the long grass for the second time this century. The cost alternatives were between £1,200,000 and £5,400,000. The money wasted would have run a much-loved local library for a year.

The words Landmark Library have cropped up time and time ago and no-one seemed to know what one was. Mr Mustard knew he had seen the detail somewhere and his alter ego being a debt collector he never forgets anything although his little grey cells work more slowly now that his brain is full of hundreds of council documents and facts and figures. His brain rolled back to the month in which he started blogging and in particular 29 March 2011 when Cabinet met and Mr Mustard sees from his diary that he was playing snooker that evening (badly!). In the Cabinet meeting the Strategic library review and its 7 recommendations were given the nod.

The report, which you can see on-line, runs to 115 pages. Here are the words that you need to know about Landmark Libraries. There is some duplication from different sections of the review.

Landmark libraries: These libraries will be amongst the busiest in London.

They will be in the busiest centres and will be on good transport routes where people regularly go.

They will have specialisms in higher education, further education and the arts and will have additional services will be available (sic) from One Barnet partners from benefits advice, CAB sessions, to additional ICT and learning lessons.

They will have:

A wide ranging, quality and comprehensive book stock

High quality children's and young people's activities, programmes, and spaces

A wide range of events and activities – reading groups, author events, learning sessions

High quality community meeting rooms and spaces

Spaces to study and relax

Longer opening hours

Landmark libraries:

1000 – 2000sqm sites, open 56.5 hours per week including Sundays.

These libraries will be located in the busiest centres and will be on good transport routes where people regularly go. Additional services will be available from One Barnet partners from benefits advice, CAB sessions, to additional ICT and learning lessons.

They will have:

A wide ranging, quality and comprehensive book stock

High quality children's and young people's activities, programmes, and spaces

A wide range of events and activities – reading groups, author events, learning sessions

High quality community meeting rooms and spaces

Spaces to study and relax

Develop a physical network based around three landmark libraries (Hendon, Finchley, Chipping Barnet); nine leading libraries; two community libraries.

Description

This option would provide an efficient, well located within Barnet, based around a network of three landmark libraries, all offering a wide range of services, colocation with sympathetic (what?) services, lengthy opening hours, well-located within the borough to attract a large user base.

All three sites would be developed over the next five years to be amongst the most successful in London.

In addition, to provide extensive coverage across the borough, a network of nine leading libraries would be maintained offering extensive stock collections, community spaces, study areas, internet access and online resources.

This could be expanded with (the) creation of a new library in Brent Cross/Cricklewood.

Link Libraries would be developed to provide a joint service with partner agencies to offer an innovative service.

A comprehensive activity programme would be developed, and community and third sector partners engaged in designing a facility to meet local needs and improve support for reading and learning.

Now go back up to the feasibility slides and see how many of them fitted into the 1,000 to 2,000 square metre range. Chipping Barnet library is Mr Mustard's nearest library and that has 1,500 square metres of space and so fits within the size definition. None of the options identified in the feasibility study were more than two thirds of the size of the 1,630 Chipping Barnet library which Mr Mustard regards as adequate rather than Landmark. Mr Mustard is now worried about the Capita Symonds costings as they have added together the 2 floors of his local library being 1070 and 560 and got the answer 1,650 instead of 1,630. How far out is their minimum cost figure of £3,300,000? Would any construction industry experts who happen to be reading confirm the price at which you could build a new library of 1,005 sq m as Mr Mustard would hazard that it would cost between £1m and £2m.

So only one option just managed to break into the size criteria and so rather than a Landmark Library ever being an option only a molehill library was even remotely on the cards. Now Mr Mustard's value for money brain is throbbing. If a Landmark Library was truly required were Crapita Symonds only asked for options that met a criteria of 1,000 sq. m. or were they simply asked what size library they could shoehorn into the artsdepot? Whose stupid idea was it to even try and put a library into this building? Was it the brainchild of Cllr Robert Rams or did someone else suggest it and he end up having to flog it (like a dead horse)? Robert, do tell.

On November 17th November there is a FREE writers workshop at the best library in town, The Friern Barnet Library and Community Hub. The workshop is by Greenacre Writers and Mr Mustard notes that they have a short story group. He hopes to get along to the workshop as he has started a short story, provisionally entitled Waaaaaaaaaah! and he needs to finish it.

Robert came home late from the council chamber & sat on the sofa sobbing. What's wrong darling, his wife asked tenderly, gently brushing the tears from his suntanned face, did your beloved football team lose again? No, whined Robert, nobody loves me. I was going to leave such a lovely legacy to people, a new library, and yet the public don't like it, I don't understand them.

I'm afraid to go to Friern Barnet because they had an effigy of me at an outdoor library which was more popular even in the pouring rain than my lovely little library inside a nice warm artsy building. They put horns on a picture of me, waaaaaaaaaah.

Oh dry your tears Robert, they were probably just having a bit of fun, they wouldn't actually harm you dear. Sticks and stones Robert said his wife whilst thinking to herself oh dear, it's words in the printed form that have got him into trouble.

Robert bleated on. Squatters have occupied my building and they are more popular than me. Waaaaaaaaaah. I asked the Court to evict them, it should have been a 5 minute job but the Judge liked them more than me and let them stay for a while. Waaaaaaaaaah.

Robert was now in full flow, waaaaaaaaaah, and, sniff, I am behind on budget he said because I have had to pay for security guards, and overtime, and extra rent, and for some consultants, and I can't sell the building, it's only an old building, it doesn't matter, waaaaaaaaaah...........

and so the story continued...........

Did it have a happy ending? Mr Mustard hasn't written the ending yet but has a funny feeling in his bones that the completed story will have a happy ending for the public who get a new extended library in Friern Barnet and an unhappy one for Robert who finds himself in 2014 once again a complete unknown and misses seeing his name in print in local blogs and being told off by an angry lady for tweeting in council meetings.

Feel free to write your own ending. Waaaaaaaaaah!

Yours frugally

Mr Mustard

Note: Any resemblance to characters living or dead is, of course, entirely coincidental.

CHAPTER 8

13 December 2012   SCRUTINY COMMITTEE

Comment from Keith Martin to the BMO Scrutiny Committee of Barnet
Council 13 December 2012

Thank you very much for allowing our questions to be broadened into
your wider debate on issues confronting the Council and the
community.
It is very heartening from the point of view outside the Council
chamber to be reminded that the principles of public service and free
debate are alive and well among some of the councillors.

I welcome what is clearly an effort to overhaul the education of some
other councillors who have been resistant to widening their horizons. It
is to these councillors that I address my comments.

1   I propose the reintroduction of the posts of
        Borough Librarian
        Borough Arts Officer and
        Borough Architect.
        The replacement is to be regretted of these senior
        advisers by outside consultants, whose lack of
        experience and local knowledge has often led them into
        giving ill-researched advice to councillors and council

staff, to the detriment of their ability to make wise decisions and pronouncements at Council meetings. I could bore you with details, but I think the point is widely understood from, for example, the bloggings of Councillor Robert Rams in his plaintive realisation that the Council library strategy for a Landmark library at artsdepot is in urgent need of revision, especially given the emergence of the reopened Friern Barnet library as an example of how libraries can become again hubs of hope in the communities which compose our borough.

2   I propose that experienced members of local society be invited to be co-opted as advisory members of council committees appropriate to their expertise and experience,
for example, libraries and arts.

This was done by Camden Council on their Libraries and Arts Sub-committee, which advised on the running of the Camden Festival. Such as Johnny Dankworth, Benny Green and the music critic Felix Aprahamian, as well as representatives from Music and Arts in Camden and Hampstead Artists Council, worked with the council staff to plan and implement a festival which was world famous, on what was a small budget of about £30,000 in the 1970s and 80s. Andrew Harper will remember being a part of it. The secret was to offer guarantees against loss to the local participants, and this enabled the small pot to go an astonishingly long way.

The shambles of Barnet's library strategy would not have happened if the advice of local experts had been actively welcomed. The farce of Public Consultation was, as has become the norm in Barnet, a wasteful exercise, the results of which were ignored by the people who wrote the Strategy. In the urgent need to rewrite it to cover current conditions, this lesson must be learned.

3   Now in mentioning this next point I realize that I must seem to be ungrateful in the extreme, because it is a criticism of some committee chairs such as the Mayor, the Leader and indeed of this committee. The point is that it is incumbent on the Chair to advise councillor colleagues and council staff, in responding to questions from fellow councillor scrutineers or public questions, to avoid making evasive replies, but to honestly answer the question to the best of their ability. An example of this lack of discipline was in the recent Scrutiny Committee on Friern Barnet library, where Cllr Brian Salinger asked for information on the probable whereabouts at artsdepot of the Landmark library, and its probable date of opening. Cllr Rams could have answered the question by quoting from the feasibility study. Instead he put Bill Murphy in to bat, who wasted everyone's time by explaining his role in

trying to implement the library budget – not a word in reply to Cllr Salinger's questions. It was this evasiveness which, quite understandably, caused Mike Gee in the public gallery to explode into criticism. So the chairs can help avoid this sort of situation.

4   To sum up, in conclusion, my recommendation to some – by no means all –
of the councillors is that you bear in mind your role as elected members to be PUBLIC SERVANTS and to place the delivery of quality PUBLIC SERVICES at all times as your highest priority. Higher than cost effectiveness, which is of little use unless accompanied by quality of service.

The strength of public opposition to the outsourcing policies encompasses concerned individuals of all parties and none, and is due largely to the insensitivity to serious and sincere concern shown by some councillors, touched sadly with a degree of arrogance. Let us hope that some lessons have been learned.

Barnet, like other councils, indeed the country, has a financial problem, but the present proposals and policy will not solve it and will emasculate our borough. There is still time to have second thoughts. Otherwise there may well arise the question of personal responsibility of individual councillors for breach of public duty.

Elected members who treat public service principally as a means towards their career development rather than a PUBLIC DUTY have misunderstood the reasons why people have elected them.

Keith Martin

13 December 2012

Reserved for Members of the Public Submitting Questions/Comments

Mr Keith Martin

BAPS TAKES OVER BARNET TOWN HALL 29
NOVEMBER 2012

CHAPTER 9

5 February 2013

We are interrupting the chronological sequence of the story to add the contribution by Reema Patel to her blog on 5 February 2013, which precedes her report on the Court case of 17 and 18 December 2012.

Reema Patel's Blog

Comment on Barnet, local government, law and politics

Final Note from the McKenzie Friend: Reflections on Community and Protest

I write this final note after a day of helping to put Friern Barnet Library in order to begin a new, exciting, dynamic and innovative chapter in its life. Tomorrow the Friern Barnet Community Library group (FBCL) will sign a licence with Barnet Council to run a community library and community centre from the premises. To track my note-taking throughout this saga of court hearings, see my **first set of notes,** my **second set of notes** and the **witness statements** in their entirety.

Friern Barnet Library, rightly, has obtained a reputation of being the library that refused to die – even as other similar libraries face closures across the country, and are fast becoming the symbol of the coalition government's drastic and indiscriminate cuts to public services. The truth is that a library encapsulates much that is valuable and beautiful about humanity, and collective action. It encapsulates the significance that access to books, education and learning can have in narrowing an ever widening gap between the rich and poor in society. It also encapsulates a commitment to social justice and to community values – the first libraries were not state-provided but evolved out of mutuals and co-operatives; they stemmed from a community-based recognition that more could be achieved for those who struggled, who were on low incomes – collectively than individually.

The library had been closed in April 2012, after a wave of protests by the Save Friern Barnet Library campaign (which had been running for over 2 years). The campaign group organised a number of innovative protests, staging a sit-in – their own 'occupation' – on the day of the closure of the library building. Between 5 April 2012 and September 2012 the building was left empty, and a promise of a new replacement 'Landmark Library' dangled in front of campaigners. That Landmark Library never appeared. On 5 September 2012 the Occupy movement reopened the library – prompting a chain of court hearings that culminated in a trial on the 17th/18th December 2012.

Many in the campaign know me as a 'legal adviser' – a McKenzie friend (I am not yet a qualified lawyer). This is my first significant court case – one that I feel so privileged to see through from 5th September up until now, where we have secured a concrete outcome for the community (a continuing library). From writing the defence, to drafting witness statements, to doing legal research on the Localism Act, chairing open meetings in the occupied library, to co-ordinating and working with the nine trustees of the new Friern Barnet Community Library, it's been something of a rollercoaster ride lurching from one stop-point to another, sometimes without an end in sight. Much of this has involved just doing one's best and trusting that eventually, insurmountable issues would resolve themselves. And by and large – they did. The final stage in my role as this McKenzie friend has included negotiating with the Council as advisor to the trustees in relation to the licence – again a strategic advisory role that had legal elements to it, but was not about legal expertise so much as finding a sensible solution for all parties. I had not expected the court proceedings to last this long. I don't think others did either – but that they lasted as long as they did is a testament to the perseverance of the campaigners. Friern Barnet Library to me is not just a local issue. It is symbolic of an awakening sense of community which has long been left dormant in Britain; a shift to a new culture and a new way of thinking about how human beings relate to each other. We have only to look at what made this campaign successful when so many others fell by the roadside to understand what is meant by this. The strength of this campaign comes from the fact that it has been deeply-rooted in the diverse communities that characterise Friern Barnet and its surroundings. Activists met in the library in order to save the library. They ran the library on a voluntary-basis – and their running the occupied library was in and of itself their protest against the council's closure itself.

When Occupy entered, they did so explicitly with the purpose of supporting the community in protest. The community responded positively – so positively that the judge in the County Court had this to say during the Council's protracted struggle to obtain a possession order against the occupiers;

43. *it is abundantly clear that the protest is still active and I am satisfied that the occupiers could make good use of the occupation in the future to promote their cause. I thus make a finding that the termination of the illegal occupancy will*

interfere with the defendant's right of freedom of expression and the right to freedom of peaceful assembly

and, where comparisons were drawn between a similar line of argument relied upon in the Occupy/St. Paul's case, (*City of London Corporation v Samede*) she said;

49. *In contrast to the St Paul's protest there is no question of these defendants causing any breach of the peace or by putting local waste disposal systems under strain. To the contrary, the defendants have by all accounts been a welcome addition to the local community and there have been no complaints about their occupancy except possibly a report when the alarm went off after the protestors went into the building.*

50. *The St Pauls protestors caused commercial damage to adjacent shops and businesses, restriction in their trade, no such complaint has been raised here. To the contrary, the positive activities at the library, including a wide-range of events have been well received by local residents. The local authority submit that the prejudice they will suffer by continued occupation relates not to these matters but to the future of this building and in particular the possible disposal of the building to a community group under the Localism Act'*

The Court of Appeal declined to hear the case on appeal. So ultimately, Council might well have won in law but they had to jump through burning hoops in order to get a possession order which ordinarily should have been available summarily. To their credit, they ultimately opted not to enforce the possession order, instead granting a licence in exchange for a seamless transition over to the trustees of Friern Barnet Community Library.

The legal proceedings – including the fantastic pro bono work by Leigh Day and by Sarah Sackman who agreed to take up the case when I approached them months ago – have been instrumental, but not the only reason for the success of the campaign. Whilst the law is a fantastic way in which levers of social change and action can be achieved, it remains a tool and a platform. In this case, it gave voice and a platform to those who had been left voiceless by a Council that refused to listen. The message was that the protest itself was the campaigners – and the campaigners' alone. Our argument was that it was the community that was protesting – and the Council, a public body under the Human Rights Act 1998, had to be mindful of any infringement of those rights – that the burden shifted to the local authority to justify its infringement of those rights.

The energy that has surrounded the library in the last few weeks has been palpable – almost electric. Tomorrow's licence-signing, farewell to the occupiers, and celebration will be the conclusion of what has been a story of conflict between Council and community.

I hope that it marks the beginning of a promising relationship between community and citizen.

It is with some sadness but also with some anticipation that I sign off this final note as FBL's McKenzie friend,

(but most certainly not signing off as a friend)

Reema.

Reema Patel's Blog

Comment on Barnet, local government, law and politics

Friern Barnet Library. The Witness Statements

At the trial on Monday 17th December 2012 Fiona Brickwood (supporter of the defendants and community), Peter Phoenix (defendant from the Occupy movement) and Keith Martin (defendant and resident who applied to be joined with the defendants) gave evidence before Barnet County Court and judge Patricia Pearl.

I had the privilege of working with them to put together their written statements. They have kindly given permission for these witness statements to be put on this blog so that residents and fellow community supporters can read these statements of support and so that what they had to say can reach a wider audience.

I've posted them up here in order of the giving of evidence.

FIONA BRICKWOOD

Ms. Brickwood

I, Fiona Brickwood of [*address not disclosed for data protection reasons*] WILL STATE AS FOLLOWS:

I make this statement in support of the defendants to the possession proceedings brought by the Claimant.

Insofar as the facts in this statement are within my knowledge they are true. Insofar as the facts in this statement are not within my direct knowledge, they are true to the best of my knowledge and belief.

I have been a resident in Friern Barnet for 16 years. I was not actively involved in any political matters until the council planned to dispose of our local library, in 2011.

Losing Friern Barnet library would be very damaging to our community. It is our only public building, so the only place where community activities can take place. A quarter of the children in our ward live in poverty. It is much harder to shift the cycle of deprivation if there is no local library.

In 2011, Barnet Council conducted a major consultation asking all Barnet residents whether they agreed the council's plans to replace Friern Barnet and North Finchley libraries with a "Landmark Library" to be built in North Finchley. 73% of respondents said they did not agree to this proposal, but the Council decided to disregard the result of their consultation and proceed with their plans to close both libraries. This created huge public protest, with two petitions presented to Cabinet and many letters to councillors and the press.

The council did not need to cut this service as the £432,000 they budgeted to receive from the sale of the library is only 0.0015% of their annual budget. The social cost to Friern Barnet of losing our library would be high, and the monetary gain to the council from disposing of this asset would be insignificant, so I believe that this plan to dispose of our library is contrary to the public interest.

In July 2011, a group of residents and local businesses, including myself, offered to develop a Neighbourhood Plan, to retain Friern Barnet library, whilst generating money to help the council's financial problems. In response to my question at a cabinet meeting on 26 July 2011, the council agreed to defer closure of the library to allow us time to develop the proposal, and promised to make their officers and resources available to work with us on this (Exhibit 1.1). Since then, our group ("Friern Barnet Co-Action"), has continued to work with various senior council officers to develop this proposal.

Friern Barnet Co-action has had various meetings with council officers to discuss and develop our proposals. The council's deadline for community proposals was extended twice, firstly to 31 December 2011 and then to 31 March 2012.

The Cabinet then decided to close the library in April this year, against the advices of its own Scrutiny Committee. However, the council has continued to work with Friern Barnet Co-Action, to develop our proposal for a Community Hub based in Friern Barnet Library.

I have supported the campaign to save Friern Barnet library since it started in the Spring of 2011. After the library was closed – against the wishes of the people and the advice of the council's Scrutiny Committee – I helped the Save Friern Barnet Library group to organise and run a 'pop up' library on the Library Green, (an open space located adjacent to the library building). I stored books, which had been donated to the pop-up library, in my home, delivered and collected them each week, and helped staff the book stalls. This "pop up" library served several purposes: it demonstrated local opposition to the closure of the library and also showed the need for a library service in the local area.

The local community has been very supportive of the campaign, especially the Royal British Legion, who are located next to the Friern Barnet Library site and who have agreed to be part of our Community Hub and Neighbourhood Plan. They supported the Pop Up Libraries by lending us tables, storing some books, providing tea for the library campaign to raise donations.

Having the pop-up library reaffirmed that the library building and the surrounding open space is land which belongs to the community, and it allowed us to assert our right to that. Barnet Council is now seeking a possession order over the open land as well as the land where the library building stands, but it is my belief that the public is entitled to use the open land beside the library building to meet, socialise and demonstrate on, and that we have a right of expression to do so.

Following the pop-up library demonstrations, the library building was occupied on 4 September 2012. At the time council was considering our application for a £40,000 grant to support our proposal. This included library facilities in Friern Barnet Library and a community-run Enterprise Hub to help people into work, funded by the profits from an Apprentice Cafe, which our group will run in a local cafe. (We are currently in discussion with the cafe owners.)

Following the occupation and reopening of the library as a library by volunteers, I attended several meetings between council officers, residents and occupiers to negotiate proposals for a library and community hub provision in Friern Barnet.

The first two meetings (10th and 17th September) were in the Friern Barnet Library building; the third meeting was at the Council's offices at North London Business Park; the fourth meeting (which I did not attend) was at the Council's site at South Friern library.

All meetings were with senior council officers. Up to thirty residents attended these meetings, with some of the occupiers including Pete Phoenix, and many long-standing campaigners for the reopening of the library including Keith Martin, Mike Gee and Rosie Canning.

We asked officers repeatedly whether the key decision maker for the libraries (Robert Rams) was available to attend the negotiations. The officers had said that they would ask him, but subsequently informed us that he was too busy to attend.

Throughout all these meetings and negotiations, we discussed our proposals to have a library on the Friern Barnet Library site itself. During our meetings, Bill Murphy stated very explicitly that he was required to produce £400,000 for the library budget, and that if this was not provided from the sale of Friern Barnet Library, that we would need to produce it in some other way. This is inconsistent with the council's offer in October 2011, where they said they would allow us to run a community-run library in Friern Barnet library, renting the building, provided this was done at 'little or no cost to the council'.

Pete Phoenix discussed with Bill Murphy being given the time to raise the £400,000 to buy back the Friern Barnet library site.

The council officers repeatedly offered the option of setting up a community-run library in Friary House.

The council have been offering us Friary House for a community-run library since July 2011. We residents have repeatedly told the council that Friary House is unsuitable for a library, because its location in the park is not fully accessible for people with disabilities, and it would be unsafe to access in the late evenings and the nights.

We also asked whether we were negotiating with the right members of staff, ie whether the council officers who were negotiating with us actually had the authority to agree to our retaining Friern Barnet library. It was confirmed to us that these decisions were in fact not in the remit of those library officers any longer as the building had moved to the remit of the property disposals team. It is not clear to me whether the officers who entered into negotiations with us intended to, or were equipped to make the decisions they needed to make to achieve a constructive solution with the community.

We had been under the impression, during our conversations with the council officers, that there would be no attempt to evict the occupiers and the library volunteers while these negotiations were ongoing. We had concluded the second meeting and had made arrangements for the third meeting when the defendants received the notice of possession proceedings. As a result we were in the odd situation of continuing to discuss proposals for the continued use and community provision of the Friern Barnet Library premises whilst they had already issued proceedings against the occupiers.

It remains my belief that as the building and especially the green space around it is land that belongs to the community, the building was given to the council for public health purposes and bought specifically for the purpose of creating a public library, that Barnet Council does not have a right to stop members of the public from using the building for community purposes or from demonstrating inside the building. It is clear that people have donated these books and given their time to the running of the community library because they want this library to remain open. They are protesting against this specific cut in the local area as well as providing a valuable service to the community. I believe that it was deeply wrong for the Council to make this cut.

Neither the pop-up libraries on the Library Green nor the volunteer library inside the Friern Barnet Library building has caused any nuisance or disturbance to others. On the contrary it is has provided a valued service to the community in a space specifically adapted to that purpose.

PETER PHOENIX

I, Peter Phoenix of *[address not
disclosed for data protection reasons]*

WILL STATE AS FOLLOWS:

I make this statement in support of my defence to the possession
proceedings brought by the Claimant.

Insofar as the facts in this statement are within my knowledge they
are true. Insofar as the facts in this statement are not within my
direct knowledge, they are true to the best of my knowledge and
belief.

Background information

I am a community activist, and a member of the Occupy
movement. I had received a phone call from the Occupy movement
who stated that they needed my help in relation to this particular
occupation. I am known as a specialist in working with community
centres, and I have experience in communicating and facilitating
dialogue between owners and occupiers – especially in working out
interim use agreements between owners and occupiers where
there are large empty buildings. For example, I have worked with
the Jewish Community Centre for London and successfully

negotiated a deal for the community, and have also worked with Circle Anglia Housing Association in negotiating housing provision for the homeless.

One of my reasons for choosing this particular building is because I believe that there remains a need for libraries as beacons of education and learning, and as institutions that provide free access to knowledge. I wanted to draw attention to the social cost of the cuts to local authority budgets, and the effect that would have on individuals. The original occupier of Friern Barnet library, Dave was once a librarian. He left after the third day of occupation but had initiated this entry into the building as he wished to reopen the library. He knew that there was a large local campaign which had hosted demonstrations outside of the library but felt that this campaign would have a stronger voice if the community could run a community library as a form of protest, and that this occupation would provide the community with a greater platform to express their opposition to this local cut to their local library.

Chronology of Events

I entered the building on the 5th September 2012 after two individuals entered before me from the Occupy movement on the 4th September 2012. I had been let in by them through the back door. The two individuals who entered before me, John and Dave, informed me that on the afternoon of the 4th September 2012 a lady from the Library Services department in Barnet Council called Heather Mills had offered the individuals another building to use. Council officers had visited them and had offered the downstairs room of Friary House, with the potential to use the upstairs rooms for the purposes of establishing and running a community library.

I asked John and Dave to take a note of what had happened. We then emailed the Council to thank them for their kind offer of use of Friary House on 5th September; and asked some questions. These were (1) how many rooms were on offer, and (2) when the move into Friary House could take place. The Council responded by email the day after (6th September 2012) where they clarified that both the upstairs and the downstairs rooms were on offer, and that before a move into the building was effected, a lengthy list of details needed to be supplied.

At this point the Council had at no stage in their discussions with us mentioned anything about our trespassing on Council property, nor did officers ask us to leave. In fact they engaged in extensive negotiations over 4 meetings, discussing financial options to run a community library.

After receiving this email, we called the Council and indicated our interest in the proposal . Heather Mills from the council asked for a meeting with Council officials including Julie Taylor – Assistant

Executive, on the following Monday 10th September at 10.00 am on the premises at Friern Barnet Library. Again, at no point at this stage in their discussions did the Council state that we were trespassers.

I then invited members of the community who had been longstanding activists for a community library in the local area to attend this meeting. 28 local residents appeared at this initial meeting, including a number of well-known Barnet bloggers as well as Keith Martin and Fiona Brickwood, all of whom have also provided their witness statements.

This meeting lasted around an hour, and I undertook to facilitate this meeting between these members of the community and the Council. There was significant anger towards council officials – primarily focused upon the fact that the Council had only agreed to consult and discuss the issue of library provision with members of the community after the occupation had happened, and had failed to enter into constructive negotiations with the community before this event. They had also ignored the response to the Library consultation where 73% of the replies said they wanted to save this library and not have the Arts Depot Landmark Library project, which has since been cancelled.

We had still not been told at this stage that we were trespassing on the property, (in fact at none of the 4 council community liaison meetings were we told that we were trespassing nor were we asked by Barnet Council to leave the building) and the Council agreed to meet with myself, the other occupiers, as well as members of the community a week later on the Friern Barnet Library premises (on 17 September 2012) to discuss proposals for the provision of library services in the local area.

Around this time myself, Mike Gee and Fiona Brickwood were shown around Friary House by Heather Mills (2nd visit of our group). I have attached photos of this extensive guided tour visit where we discussed in detail rooms possible to be used, marked Exhibit 1.1.

There were around 25 members of the community at this second meeting. I continued to facilitate the meeting. At this meeting we agreed to discuss some proposals for library provision which were on the table. We were informed by Mr.Cooper from the property services department that the library was not to be used yet for a period of six to eighteen months.

We discussed with the Council the interim use of Friern Barnet library as a community/council run and volunteer run library at low cost. At the third meeting (24.09.2012) with Council officers which was held at Council offices in North London Business Park, seven or eight members of the community were present.

in our discussions with council officers Bill Murphy and Mike Fahey from Library Strategy, a number of proposals were considered which involved Friern Barnet Library.

A revenue/rental option

A purchase for £400,000 option

A completely voluntary run library option, with £10,000 and 10,000 books as well as integration into the library computer system.

Mike Fahey mentioned that the council did options appraisals, so we supplied them with our own options document by the next week outlining 9 possible variable proposals.

Bill Murphy (Library Strategy) stated that if the community could raise an estimated £30,000 – £40,000 of revenue for the rental of Friern Barnet library, that would enable the Council to borrow the £400,000 it needed to keep the library open, and to make up for the identified deficit that the sale of the building was intended to solve.

The Council had offered £10,000, along with 10,000 books to fund a volunteer-run community library. We then emailed the Council and asked them whether the £10,000 offered could be subtracted from the £30-40,000 to reduce the sum that needed to be raised to £20,000-30,000. I then estimated on a rough spread sheet how that revenue of £400-600/week could be generated to enable the library to remain open and provided this estimate to council officers.

This offer was again made by the community and by the occupiers to the Council at the fourth meeting at the South Friern Library building on 10th October 2012. The council officer in question responded that he would have to 'ask whether there is a political will' to accept the proposal where the community raised between £30,000-40,000 for the library to remain open.

Bill Murphy said that the council was very eager to engage with the New Carnegie Foundation who may have been able to raise significant funds to purchase this building and open other Academy Buildings, as they had the backing of several American millionaires.

Bill Murphy said that the council was most interested in Option 4 – the purchase of the building for £ 400,000 and that if we produced this we could have the building.

We agreed to have a 5th meeting. However, the Council officials noted that meeting the following week would clash with the possession proceedings and the court hearing so they agreed to meet the week after the possession proceedings. Mike Fahey said he would check the availability of the room in South Friern Library for the week after the court case.

This meeting never happened. We feel we were significantly close to finding a mutually beneficial solution for community and council and would like more time to find a resolution. We have made an offer to enter mediation with the help of Berkeley Square professional mediators but this offer was declined.

The Council's application for a possession order ran completely counter to the fact that the Council had asked us to enter into negotiations about the use of Friern Barnet Library, and had never explicitly told us that we were trespassing on the premises whilst the library was being used and operated as a community library.

In fact, our ability to run the library seemed to form the basis and reason for their ongoing discussions and negotiations with us as they saw that there was an opportunity to work with us to provide volunteer-run services at a low cost in order to meet their statutory obligations.

Conclusion

I believe that not only did Barnet Council grant us an implied licence to be on the property while they were commencing possession proceedings, but also that pursuing a possession order itself interferes with the community's right to be on the premises in order to effect a strong protest.

I believe that this is the Council's sole reason for seeking possession and that there is no justification for interfering with this right to community protest and individual expression. The grant of a possession order will interfere with the right to protest.

The level of media coverage and the platform that this occupation has given individuals has meant that the community and community groups have support that they would not otherwise have had.

They have been covered in national media; such as the Guardian, the Independent and the Daily Mirror, BBC,ITV and has received significant attention on television and radio (including German television, and French/Swedish radio).

It has enabled the community to express their support for the library through donating over 8000 books, as well as volunteering to fill in a community librarians rota and through using the library. The location of the occupation of Friern Barnet Library and the way in which the community has registered its protest against the library closure by operating the library is critical to the message we wish to the send to the Council. There have been many very well attended community talks, workshops and discussions in the library building.

It has also enabled the community to provide a library service to themselves – something that is currently not being provided as a consequence of the closure of Friern Barnet Library. The operation of the library is not causing any nuisance or interference to others.

We have also recently heard that the proposals for a substitute library at the Arts Depot in Finchley have been shelved which has implications for the Council's statutory duty to provide an efficient and comprehensive library service under the Museums and Libraries Act 1964.

We are, in effect, through running a community library – stepping in to make up for the Council's failure to meet its statutory obligations.

KEITH MARTIN

Mr. Martin

I, Keith Martin of *[address not disclosed for data protection reasons]* WILL STATE AS FOLLOWS:

I make this statement in support of my defence to the possession proceedings brought by the Claimant.

Insofar as the facts in this statement are within my knowledge they are true. Insofar as the facts in this statement are not within my direct knowledge, they are true to the best of my knowledge and belief.

I have been a long-standing campaigner for the reopening of, and against the closure of Friern Barnet Library. I participated in both the pop up demonstrations and in the sit in at the Friern Barnet Library which had been hosted by the local Save Friern Barnet Library Campaign Group. Both the consultation and the wider library strategy showed how unpopular the closure of the local library was – as did the continued campaign against its closure, and the campaign to reopen the library. By protesting on the grass beside the library building, the community continuously demonstrated that it had a point to make and that it would continue to use public land in order to make that point. Furthermore, by protesting inside the building by using what was once an empty disused space to run a community library, the community has also demonstrated that it had a point to make against this cut to the library service. It has done so by contributing, volunteering for, and donating to the on-going running of the library service.

It is my understanding that this library was given to the people of Friern Barnet with the support of the Carnegie Foundation. The Carnegie Foundation donated money for the provision of library services in the local area. I believe that Barnet Council have no right to close the library, and that the people of Friern Barnet have the right for the site to be continued to be used for community purposes and as a library.

I attended three out of the four negotiations which took place. These were mainly chaired by the lead occupant Pete Phoenix. I believe that Pete Phoenix has great ability to enable effective dialogue to take place between the Council and the community. We had asked him if he would be willing to facilitate these discussions and he said he would be happy to do so.

I attended both of the negotiations at Friern Barnet Library itself. I also attended the fourth negotiation at the South Friern Library premises. I can confirm that Rosie Canning, another long-standing activist, was there and took detailed minutes of the first two meetings which are a permanent record of the discussions between Council officers and the team who were negotiating on behalf of the community. Roger Tichborne took minutes of the fourth meeting. These negotiations included myself, Peter Phoenix who is the main occupant of the library, Rosie Canning, Fiona Brickwood, Mike Gee, and some local bloggers – such as Roger Tichborne who runs a blog called 'The Barnet Eye', and Theresa Musgrove, who runs a blog under the alias of 'Mrs Angry'. After the second meeting some of us met with council officers at Friern Barnet Library and travelled to Friary House for a viewing of the site. This was offered to us in exchange for the occupiers ceasing the occupation. We declined the site for several reasons. One was that it was not accessible as it was in a dark and unlit area. Another was that we knew that it had been intended to be rented to the police and was a building designed for police and not library use. We also knew that there were some South Asian community groups within the building (which is used at an almost maximum capacity) and we were not clear where they would go, or when a library would be available on those premises.

The first meeting at Friern Barnet Library did not rule out the possibility that the community library would continue to run on the premises with the consent of the Council. There were several options that were on the table – and one suggestion provided by Julie Taylor who is the Assistant Chief Executive of Barnet Council, was the site at Friary House. Phoenix accepted that this was a possible option. However, Friern Barnet Library ruled out.

At the first meeting the local blogger Roger Tichborne asked Craig Cooper (a representative from the Property/Estates department at Barnet Council) whether the building remained within the remit of Cllr Robert Rams. He responded that it was 'no longer a library, it was an asset'. It is my belief that Barnet Council were not genuinely interested in negotiating to keep the library open. When the occupiers learnt that a possession order would be sought and that papers had been filed for eviction, this came as a complete surprise as we had agreed to continue negotiating. This behaviour was completely at odds with the dialogue and mediation which had been taking place between council officers and residents/occupiers at the meetings about the provision of library services. I did not feel that this was the act of an honest negotiator. I believe also that council officers made statements implying a promise not to issue proceedings. Julie Taylor had promised to convey to councillors the views of those who met that negotiations should be continued between the council and the community. She had said 'I can guarantee you, that I will put that point of view to the councillors.' It had also been stated that 'no snap decisions would be made', when local blogger Theresa Musgrove asked as to whether the Council would be seeking possession.

There was therefore an implication here that the Council would not torpedo negotiations by applying for a possession order or eviction proceedings, especially as the main occupant (Pete Phoenix) was by this point recognized as essential to facilitating the negotiations by both sides. The council then continued to offer to meet with the community group and with the occupants including myself to negotiate for the provision of library services after the papers for possession had been issued. Negotiations have now ceased.

I am, as well as a witness, a defendant. I wanted to add my name to the list of defendants as I wished Barnet Council to know that their action was not simply against non-residents of Barnet but also against long standing residents and the council taxpayer. I have supported this occupation and have joined my name as a co-defendant to this action because I wish to refute any suggestion that the defendants comprise of non-residents only, to refute the suggestion that the Council is merely taking action against individuals, rather than the community. I join my name to the defendants on behalf of the local community as a long standing activist.

The local community want this library to be reopened, and have continuously been protesting against its closure through the act of using the library itself, donating to the library and volunteering to run the community library.

—

All of the witness statements above were signed and dated 14th November 2012.

Thanks go to an immense campaign and to other activists who were integral to the campaign and to the case. We wouldn't be here without the ongoing campaigning and support of the **Save Friern Barnet Library Group**. A special shout goes out to **Rosie Canning**, responsible for taking many of the minutes in the interactions between the Council and occupiers/residents and for so much of the hard work and co-ordination behind the campaign's scenes, to Mike Gee for so much of his practical dedication and perseverance – and for putting his back out in looking after the building!

Thanks goes out also to Cllrs Barry Rawlings and Pauline Coakley-Webb for their support of the community in this campaign.

A special thanks also goes out to Rabbi Jeffrey Newman who worked so hard to facilitate mediation between the parties

CHAPTER 10

THE COURT CASE

Tuesday, 18 December 2012

The People's Library: a day in court

Barnet County Court usually deals with family cases, small claims cases: routine, personal issues, attended by the plaintiffs and their legal advisers, dealt with quietly, discreetly: no one else's business, unremarked, and unreported.

Today was different. Today was when the very interesting matter of the occupation of Friern Barnet Library - the People's Library - was brought before the judge, to decide whether or not Barnet Council should be granted leave to repossess the building and evict the occupiers and community activists who have installed themselves in the library, reclaiming it for the people of Friern Barnet.

The people of Friern Barnet came to the court in large numbers today to show their support for the occupiers, crowding out the courtroom, and politely taking their turns in sitting in limited space available throughout the hearing. Politeness, and a very British attitude is the prevailing quality of the occupation, in fact, confounding almost everyone's prejudices about squatters, the occupy movement, and direct action initiatives. Here in this most British of environments, a courtroom, where justice is blind, and allocated on the basis of merit, not privilege, or force, there was perhaps the right home for much of what drives the continuing story of this small scale revolution in a library, in the heart of Tory Barnet.

The motives of the residents and activists pursuing this course of action are, in Mrs Angry's eyes anyway absolutely just, and seeking only what is fair. It is the corrupt, illegitimate authority of Barnet Council which is on trial, and called to answer for its immorality and betrayal of the best interests of the people it was elected to represent.

Judge Patricia Pearl spent most of the morning deciding on the proper way to conduct the case, and the outlines of the different arguments to be brought by the council and the defendants who are in occupation of the library. Some of the discussions were rather prolonged, and nitpicking, and the judge herself wondered if members of the public would think they were debating 'the number of angels that could be safely accommodated on the head of a pin'. Eventually proceedings got under way, with four individuals listed as the representatives of the occupiers: Peter Phoenix, Daniel Gardner, Petra Albert and Keith Martin.

For Barnet the barrister was a Mr Nicholas Grundy, and for the occupiers, Miss Sarah Sackman.

First to take the stand was an officer from property services, Susannah Lewis, who was questioned about such matters as whether or not sleeping in a library, as the occupiers do, constituted a form of residency, and therefore some sort of breach of planning regulations. It appeared that might be the case. She did admit, however, that there had been no impediment to inspection of the premises by the council's representatives by the occupiers.

Bill Murphy, a consultant working as Barnet's Assistant Director of Customer Services, and therefore ultimately responsible for libraries, was sworn in next. Incidentally, there were no Tory councillors present: scared off, no doubt, after last time, when a solitary member,, deputy leader Councillor Dan Thomas had the uncomfortable experience of being surrounded by the dozens of library supporters.

Mr Murphy said that the council had wanted to enter discussions with the occupiers and campaigners 'in good faith'. Rather puzzlingly he claimed that the council had appointed a named officer to deal with residents and campaigners over the library issue. No one in the courtroom had heard of this individual.

Some discussion ensued as to whether or not the occupiers had been informed that they were 'trespassers'. He thought that this was 'implied'.

Mr Grundy suggested that the occupation was an obstruction in the marketing of the library to community bidders, now that the building had been listed, under the new terms of the localism act, as a community asset. That was correct, said Mr Murphy.

Mrs Angry tried to understand the point being made here: that the fact that residents had taken steps to get their library building listed in this way was preventing residents from acquiring it for community use?

Mention now was made of the meeting in the occupied library on September 10th, a meeting attended by an assortment of officers, occupiers, residents, campaigners - and bloggers, including Mrs Angry.

Minutes from this meeting had been supplied, and rather bizarrely Mr Grundy, on behalf of the authority, quoted the words of John Dix, blogger Mr Reasonable, saying that the officers present were not authorised to make decisions and asking where were the councillors ... this was represented by Mr Grundy as in some way reinforcing the argument that the meeting was not to be taken as any sort of formal negotiation, or recognition of any license to occupy the premises.

It was established now that freelance journalist, Diane Taylor, also present at the 'circle of friends' meeting had asked 'will you enter into a caretaker arrangement'. The answer had been 'we will not enter into any snap decisions'.

This, you might think clearly suggested that a caretaker arrangement was therefore not ruled out as a possibility, and arguably gave legitimacy to the occupation, allied with the absence of any mention of the term 'trespass'.

Mr Murphy thought the confusion arose from the difficulty of the council's position, being 'between a rock and a hard place', and not wishing to 'make the situation worse'. He also commented that they were not dealing with 'amateur squatters' - the implication being they knew the position without it being spelt out.

After lunch, it was time for campaigner Fiona Brickwood to take the stand. Ms Brickwood is a psychotherapist by profession, and a resident of Friern Barnet for sixteen years. Her testimony was measured, convincing and yet forthright. She said she was very upset by the closure of the library, the heart, she said, of Friern Barnet. She had her own campaign group, the Friern Barnet Co-action group, but also helped with the Save Friern Library Group, being involved in protests, attending council meetings, the pop up libraries, all in order to support the community, which had rallied around, brought books, and turned it into a thriving concern. Not just donating books: computers, time, everyone coming together. People got to meet neighbours, and support each other.

Fiona listed some of the many varied activities in the occupied library: children's activities (supervised by CRB checked volunteers) social events, music, yoga, pilates, language lessons. She explained how she felt it was right to protest very strongly about the library being closed, and explained that when asked about the proposal, people had said very strongly 'no, we don't want this'.

The council's barrister made the mistake of mentioning the failure by campaigners to apply for a Judicial Review. Fiona Brickwood pointed out that in fact this was entirely due to the campaigners being misled by officers as to the process of negotiation in which they thought they were involved, which, prolonged as it was, conveniently(for the council) took them beyond what they later discovered was the three month limit for application for JR. She described this behaviour by the council as 'reprehensible'. Bill Murphy shook his head.

Asked how she felt about the occupation, Fiona said that the campaigners were 'enormously grateful' to them. As to the issue about whether trespass was mentioned, she felt that the council was 'talking through their actions', in other words effectively giving a form of legitimacy to the occupation by their negotiations.

Mr Grundy now tried to put the case that the occupation somehow disadvantaged any other groups who wished to bid to take over the library building now it was listed as a community asset. Fiona refuted this, pointing out the library had been empty for a long time, and as to any potential bids - bring'em on ...

Next up was Phoenix, the spokesperson of the library occupiers. He described himself as a community organiser of some 20 years experience - since the Rio summit of 1992. He described coming to Friern Barnet and being struck by the lack of transparency and lack of communication by the council in its dealings with residents over the library.

He wanted to enable a better dialogue, and bring the council and local community together. In his statement he had described the various activities that have taken place in the occupied library, and added a few more recent examples - the visit and reading from Will Self, an event on climate debate with the new Green Party leader, a talk by a senior Unison officer on 'transition towns'.

Holding these events, he said, demonstrated that it is a vibrant centre for the community. It strengthened the protest, raised massive awareness in the media - and as he later explained he wanted to draw attention to the wider issue of library closures. He saw himself as a facilitator for the local community, who could create a solution.

Mr Grundy wanted to know if he was a 'professional occupier'. Phoenix thought a better term would be an 'experienced occupier'.

Mr Grundy wanted to know if he thought he was good at it. Phoenix thought he was good at 'community projects'.

Mr Grundy asked him about the new listing as a community asset, implying that this meant the building would now be retained for community use. No, said Phoenix, who is no fool: this means only that retaining it is just one option.

Mr Grundy gave up.

Finally came the turn of resident Keith Martin. Keith described himself as a retired chartered accountant, and a resident of Friern Barnet for forty two years. He was involved, he said, to refute the idea that the occupiers were 'fly by nights'. It was important to protest about the library closure because Friern Barnet was not a very well off community, the local children could not easily get to another library in North Finchley, not cross the North Circular to the South Friern branch.

Keith mentioned his six hour occupation of the library on the last day of opening, and the consequent pop up libraries. The judge asked how long these continued - all through the August rain? Yes. After describing the occupation as a well run , happy place, Judge Pearl was offered a cup of tea at the library, by Phoenix, which she declined, albeit with a fair degree of amusement.

After a short break, the hearing resumed on a rather broader level of debate: the question, as raised by the occupiers barrister, of the human rights aspect of the case. And this is where the hearing stopped being about the closure of one library, and about something more intangible, and indefinable.

Articles 10 and 11 of the Human Rights Act refer to the freedom of expression, and to the right to peaceful assembly and association with others. Were these rights engaged in the context of the occupied library, and would they be infringed by eviction?

With such rights, said the judge - once they're there, they're there ...

A fascinating discussion then ensued between the two counsels and the judge on previous cases involving occupation, protest, and rights in law. The Occupy movement at St Paul's, the Peace Camp/Democratic Village on Parliament Square Gardens, and even the women's camp at Aldermaston: all these notable precedents raised and compared to the occupation of a small branch library in leafy Friern Barnet.

Would the removal of the protest represent 'an interference' with the rights expressed in law? Is a possession order an interference?

Is it not just a case of whether rights would be infringed, not just in terms of the right to expression and association, but the rights endowed in the manner of the protest itself.

Miss Sackman was now elaborating eloquently on her theme: she maintained that 'the manner and form is the protest itself ' in other words, the medium, in this context, is the message, and should be respected as the act of expression which the Article is meant to protect. An occupation to protest about the occupation of a library should be allowed to be expressed in situ, just as the Aldermaston occupation was allowed to take place in a specific location.

Since the early days of the campaign to save Friern Barnet library it has been apparent that this particular story is more than the tale of one library, or even One Barnet. It has a resonance, a significance beyond the immediate relevance of the closure of a much loved community resource. It is symbolic of something else, something harder to identify, or define. It speaks to some sort of archetypal emotion, a subconscious longing to retain something slipping just out of reach, something precious, and irreplaceable. We don't know what it is, yet, but we will do, once it has gone.

Don't take our library away: don't shut our museums. Don't sell our local services to Capita and tell us it's all for our own good: this is our community, and we want to live there in our own way, without you telling us how, or why, or what we can say, and when.

Freedom of speech, freedom of association: democratic liberties we take for granted, until they are taken away - here in Broken Barnet, we are fighting to take control of our local democracy, and our rights in law, and whatever happens tomorrow, we will continue the fight.

The People's Library: today's verdict

Posted byMrs
AngryatTuesday,
December 18, 2012

Occupier Phoenix after the
hearing, interviewed by
Australian radio news

We returned to court today to hear the verdict on the application
made by Barnet Council to claim possession of the occupied library
in Friern Barnet - the People's Library. Judge Patricia Pearl warned
the court that it would take an hour to read out her findings.

The judge repeated her observation of the previous day in which
she noted that the library supporters had been 'most co-operative

and peaceful both in and around the court'. She also remarked on the widespread media interest - local, national, and international - that the case had attracted.

Judge Pearl then proceeded to read the details of her judgement, starting with a history of the library campaign, and all the events leading up to the present occupation and consequent application from the local authority to claim possession of the building.

There were two main arguments under consideration: whether or not the council had effectively given the occupiers license to remain, and whether or not the repossession of the library would constitute a breach of the human rights act, in particular Articles 10 and 11, dealing with the right to freedom of expression, and the right to peaceful assembly and association with others.

Next the judge dealt with the listing of the library under the provisions of the new localism act, as a community asset, meaning that if the council tries to sell it, it must first consider bids from community groups.

Returning to the issue of whether or not the human rights of the protestors would be infringed by a repossession order, it was agreed that removal from the library would constitute an infringement, but that this was qualified by the greater risk of prejudicing the authority's obligation to offer the vacant property to local community groups who may wish to exercise their right to bid for the building, under the terms of the localism act. Such an infringement, in other words, is justified.

To a lay person sitting in the court, this seemed to be an extraordinary decision, in two ways: first of all that Articles 10 and 11, regarding the fundamental rights to freedom of expression, peaceful assembly and association are considered to carry less weight than a newly enacted requirement for local authorities in the UK, and second that the purpose of the community asset listing was being applied, seemingly perversely, against the very circumstance it was supposed to facilitate - by acting in good faith to protect the library from sale by Barnet Council, the campaigners were punished by losing their right to remain in the very building they were seeking to secure for the community.

By the logic of this judgement, if the campaigners had not had the building listed, presumably they would have been left in occupation, their rights to protest protected by Articles 10/11.

Except of course that Barnet's use of the community asset listing was totally cynical, and presented a convenient line of challenge. There never has, and never will be any real desire on behalf of the authority to allow a community group to take control of this building. The council will go through the pretence of entertaining bids from community groups, and find reasons to reject them, and then put the building on the open market, ready for the highest bidder. The property is worth an awful lot more than any price any local group could afford.

But all is far from lost: the judge has required that enforcement of the possession order must not be enacted before the end of a six week period, and local campaigners will hope to apply for a license to remain in the library as interim caretakers, which of course the council will do everything to avoid.

More importantly, today's judgement will be the subject of an application to the Court of Appeal, and the defendant's legal team appears confident of having a strong case to present.

Library campaigner and defendant Keith Martin leaves court unbowed - and relieved that Barnet Council did not press for costs ... More tomorrow: Mrs Angry has had more than enough of today, in all sorts of ways.

Posted by Mrs Angry at Tuesday, December 18, 2012

THE BARNET EYE
The Original and the best !!!
Beware of pale imitatations and the
invisible men

Monday, 17 December 2012

Friern Barnet Library Court Case - Day 1

I spent the day at Barnet County Court observing the proceedings as Barnet Council began their court case to evict the Friern Barnet Peoples Library.

The proceedings started with lengthy legal debates as to whether the defence could alter their hearing to include a defence that the eviction would breach article 10 & 11 of the European Human rights act. These protect the right of free speech and freedom of assembly. Not being a lawyer, the nuances of it passed me by.

Barnet Council opened by saying it was too late to include these arguments. The judge offered an adjournment. Suddenly it became alright and there was enough time. Then there was discussion as to whether Barnet may get a possession order, but allow the Peoples library to stay until the end of January. As no one trusts Barnet to do the decent thing and negotiate in good faith, this seems a bit of a non starter (although the judge seemed to like the idea). The defence seemed to suggest and adjournment of decision until the end of January may be in order.

Once all of the legal points were sorted out, amid much whinging from the Barnet Council Lawyer that the defence hadn't given him enough time and a lengthy and pointless debate about who was a defendant, Barnet Council put up their two star witnesses.

The first was Suzanna Lewis, who I believe is a former estate agent, who advises the Council on its commercial property portfolio. She made a bad start. When asked to confirm her name, she said "erm, Susan Ellis". She then got very flustered and the judge, who appears to be very jovial, got her a drink of water and asked her to sit down for a minute. The prosecution then asked some nice questions (she's on their team, so he clearly would). The Defence lawyer then started. She wasn't quite so nice. Poor Ms Lewis (or is that Ellis), was very flustered, but had to admit that the Council have been able to get access to the Library whenever they wanted and that the occupation had not actually caused any problems. She got off the stand and seemed highly relieved to still be alive. The judge clearly felt sorry for her and did at one point suggest that the prosecution barrister be a bit nicer to her.

Next up was the assistant director responsible for libraries. His name is Bill Murphy. I got a little bit cross with Bill (although I couldn't say anything). He wasn't quite as straightforward with his account of the meetings between residents and Council officials as he could have been. I was there so I probably had a little bit of a better insight into how he was spinning the facts than the judge. Given that the Council had opened by saying the occupiers of the library had no case for defence, I was puzzled as to why he was so economical with the facts.

We then adjourned. I had a conversation with Bill. He is a consultant and he's off in March. This means that whoever comes in will have no clue as to what has been going on. Bill is proud of his achievements in Barnet. He said "I've done what I can, you don't realise the pressures. We need money to run the service and we are suffering cuts". I then pointed out that they had done nothing about my suggestion in September that they start friends groups for the libraries. His response "I have lots of other things to do" and listed an impressive list. I retorted by saying that this meant the council was under resourced and clearly needed more staff. I've met people from all walks of life. It is clear to me that Bill is not on the side of the people who pay his wages. I'm sure he's a nice bloke if you are a friend of his, but he is doing the people of Barnet no favours. He clearly knows what is going on *and his performance on the stand was rather upsetting, if not entirely unexpected.*

After lunch we had the defence witnesses. First up was Fiona Brickwood from the campaign looking to run a community hub at the library. Until this point I was worried that the defence was not getting the better of the arguments (in the minds of people unfamiliar with the whole story). Any impartial observer (and quite clearly the Council team) would conclude that Fiona wiped the floor with Mr Grundy (the Barrister for the Council). She was superb. When a witness cares about an issue, is intelligent, well informed and tells the truth, they have a massive advantage. Every ruse Mr Grundy tried to use to unsettle her failed and as his Zeppelin crashed a look of abject horror appeared on the fresh face of the legal officer from Harrow who was sitting next to me. His foot started to shake at one point. I was a bit worried a puddle would appear on the floor. His colleague had nicked my seat in the lunch interval and informed Rosie from the Save FBL campaign that "they were unreserved seats". I was mildly put out until I realised I could read all the texts she was sending over her shoulder. I thoroughly enjoyed that. Most amusing. I will spare her blushes here, but the info is filed away ! Memo to any naive council officers - if you are texting, don't sit next to a nosey blogger, wind them up and then forget they are looking over your shoulder (For the absence of doubt, I am actually slightly short sighted and couldn't have read a word on the screen which was about 4 ft away. In fact even if I could see the letters, I wouldn't have bothered. I just wanted to make our friends at the council aware that they should be a bit more circumspect in their behaviour, which in the particular context, I thought was a bit stupid and careless. There are many cases of public servants being "lazy" with regards to data security, they really must think about such issues. I once worked at a company, where our salesman sat opposite two employees of a rival company discussing a bid he was working. Needless to say, this was very useful and our company won the bid. I personally respect people's privacy, which is why I used the word "could". This is rather different in its meaning to "did").

Next up was Pete Phoenix, the front man of Occupy in Barnet. Mr Grundy suggested he was a "professional activist". Mr Phoenix objected as he said he doesn't get paid. At the suggestion of the Judge, experienced was deemed a better term. Mr Phoenix explained how marvellous the reopened library was. Strangely Mr Grundy didn't disagree. In fact Mr Grundy seemed to use the defence that Mr Phoenix had done too good a job and further protests were unnecessary. All rather odd.

Last up was Barnet resident Keith Martin. The judge seemed to approve of Mr Martin. He's a retired accountant. She shared his passion for the 43 bus. Mr Grundy again tried to portray Mr Martin as a dangerous subversive, but by now his heart wasn't in it.

We had a five minute recess, then the summing up. Mr Grundy said that because Occupy had been slung out of St Pauls Courtyard by the Court of Appeal, the Judge had no choice but to do the same at the Library. The defence Barrister read out a list of "aggravating facts" at St Pauls, sited as the key facts that didn't exist in Friern, such as public nuisance, blocking the highway, health concerns, preventing people going to church. She explained that the Prosecution had conceded that the protestors at the Library were covered under articles 10 & 11 of the EHR act. The point was agreed to it was just deciding how to balance their rights with those of the council. The Council defence seems to be that there may be an as yet unidentified community group, who may wish to use the building but are deterred by the protest. Given that no such group has been identified, it is a rather shaky reason in my opinion.

We reconvene at noon tomorrow to get the judgement or determination. I suspect that the minimum the defence will get is a stay of execution until the end of January to try and sort out a proper license for the building. If I were the judge, I'd adjourn the decision until the end of January and say that if either side doesn't act in good faith that will colour the determination. The only valid concern is that if another group did appear, the council may not be in a position to evict the current occupiers if the case is struck out completely.

The real shame is that Barnet Council have scored a massive own goal. They could have got a huge level of good will and a library with far lower running costs than before had they embraced the Save Friern Barnet group's proposals. As it is we've had four days in court and a pointless and expensive legal case.

On Friday night I performed a set of music at the Library with my band the False Dots, as part of an open mic night. We had young and old, people with learning difficulties and people without. A great night was had by all. This was a true community event. Here's a video shot of the last two numbers in our set.

Friern Barnet Library Court Case Day #2

So we all trudged back at High Noon (Do not forsake me oh my Darlin') to hear Judge Pearl's decision. The reading of the judgement took approximately an hour. It was a very long and detailed analysis, which I won't bore you with the details of. The judge basically said that granting a possession order would infringe the rights of protestors as defined in Sections 10 & 11 of the Human rights act, but this was outweighed by the requirement of the council to be able to market the building in a fair and proper manner. The possession order was granted with the caveat that the council had to try and negotiate a license with campaigners to allow the people's library to continue in a volunteer manner until such time as new tenants were found.

The defendants asked for leave to appeal the decision. Judge Pearl announced that it was not in her remit to grant or block this. It looks like we'll all be doing this again at the appeal court.

It goes without saying that I believe this whole court case to be a massive own goal. The case has galvanised local support behind the library and the council has been made to look completely out of touch. In September, when the council first found out that the library was occupied, meetings were held and progress was made towards a solution. This halted abruptly when lawyers advised the officials holding the talks that they couldn't continue. With today's judgement, it is likely that the process will be restarted.

The only difference will be that thousands of pounds have been wasted on a trial and maybe thousands more on an appeal.

One small item which Barnet must be given credit for was the decision not to pursue one of the defendants, Keith Martin for costs. I sincerely hope that the dialog can be restarted in a proper spirit and a temporary license concluded to allow continuation of the People's library. Barnet Council may have won a battle, but a consensual agreement may mean we all win the war, keep a local resource and save a fortune in legal costs.

Posted by Rog T at Tuesday, December 18, 2012

Friern Barnet Library Court Case - my final thoughts

Today as I stood watching the Judge read her summing up of the reasons behind her judgement, I looked across at the various protagonists in the court. We had Mr Grundy, the council for Barnet, presumably a man who commands a few hundred pounds an hour for his services (assuming he's any good). We had Bill Murphy, the highly paid contractor who has come in on a wage perhaps equivalent to four or five librarians, to dismantle the library service. We have Suzanna Lewis, the lady who is the property specialist for Barnet. I've no idea what she gets paid. Possibly more than a librarian?

Then I looked at the other side. Keith Martin, a retired accountant who stuck his neck on the line financially to defend a library, a *man who spends his life publishing books on topics of local interest. Pete Phoenix, a community activist working to assist people who are homeless find some sort of accommodation and in Friern Barnet to stop the council from closing a library, giving of his time for free. We had a stack of other people giving up a days work and pay. Why? To defend their community.*

Yesterday I had a chat with Bill Murphy. He claimed that he isn't the bad guy. He claimed he's doing his best in a difficult circumstance. I genuinely believe that he thinks he is. The trouble is, who does he think he's doing his best for? The pensioners who use Friern Library? The children who are deprived of books? The students deprived of a place to study? Bill, do you think you have served these people, at the bottom rung of society? Those who won't earn in ten years what you earn from the taxpayer this year?

Today I also had a nice little chat with Mr Grundy. Mr Grundy clearly has had a very good education. I wondered if he has ever struggled to study in a cramped flat, surrounded by siblings with the television blaring? Maybe he has? I wondered whether he ever took refuge in a public library when he was taking his law exams. When he was at whichever Inn he is a member of, scoffing the requisite number of dinners and drinking the requisite bottles of plonk, did he ever worry about how he'd get access to the books to pass his exams? Maybe he did, I have no idea. Mr Grundy is clearly a far more clever chap than I am. He's far better spoken and I'm sure that as a trained advocate, he can earn far more money than I can. I'm sure that being highly intelligent and not dyslexic, he could write a far better, funnier and more informative blog than I can, if he chose to. Perhaps he has a social conscience and is a far better person than I am as well. Maybe, but he has done a terrible thing. He has facilitated a judgement which could lead to the closure of a community resource, depriving hundreds of people of a valued space, which may allow them to improve the quality of their education, their employment prospects and their children's well being. Mr Grundy has climbed a ladder and achieved a job with stability, good prospects, a good salary and a nice pension. He is happy to take that ladder away from a whole community of other people. He sits atop the apple tree, eating the ripe apples and tossing down the ones with worms in, to the paupers below saying "I have succeeded, but you do not deserve your library, you do not deserve the chance to better yourself, you do not deserve an opportunity to improve your prospects" because this is the effect of the judgement on all those people who need the facilities and the space to study. To Mr Grundy it is simply a job well done. I congratulate Mr Grundy on doing such a fine job. On Thursday morning, I will be down at the homeless charity where I volunteer, making toast for the homeless of London. For all Mr Grundy's wit, wealth and charm, I'd rather be there than spend another second in his company. An unkind comment was left on a picture of the gig my band did at Friern Barnet Library concerning the smell of homeless people. I would rather breathe that than share my oxygen with people who rake in huge amounts of money from destroying the quality of life of their fellow man and pulling up the ladder so the hard working, intelligent young people from poor backgrounds in Friern Barnet suffer social exclusion.

As for Ms Lewis. Presumably if she does a really good job, she'll sell the site to a property developer who will make a few million quid from it. A community will have lost its heart and someone with perhaps no association at all with Barnet will rake in a huge profit. I hope she's well paid. I hope that she is completely heartless and doesn't care at all about this, because if she does have a heart, sooner or later she is going to feel very bad about what she's done. I wouldn't wish such a pained soul on anyone.

What all of us forget sometimes is that one day, we may well be old and infirm. Money comes and money goes. The friends we have when we are doing well, disappear when times get rough. Ill health robs the strongest of us of our dignity and our authority. They say that only the good die young. Maybe the real curse for those who rape our public services is that they will have to grow old and lonely in the world they created. I remember seeing my mother on a geriatric ward in Barnet following a stroke. The forlorn stares of the patients staring out of the window was quite the saddest thing I've ever seen. For those of us who have tried to do our bit to preserve and improve our community, we will at least have consolation that we tried to make a difference, tried to do the right thing. I shudder to think what those of us who have spent our lives ripping apart communities think about when they find themselves in that position?

As they say, only the good die young. Perhaps that is the curse that the rest of us must face. A life of impotence at the hands of an uncaring state, knowing that it is partially our fault for colluding with the system that created it.

Posted by Rog T at Wednesday, December 19, 2012

CHAPTER 11

3 JANUARY 2013   THE AFTERMATH

On Christmas Day Friern Barnet Community Library was open to serve Christmas lunch to the squatters and the community; perhaps the only library in Europe to do so. The meal was delicious, especially the moussaka cooked jointly by Tirza Waizel, an Israeli Jew, and her partner Ron Cohen. What an appropriate expression of goodwill and international cooperation!

The intervention of Christmas gave Barnet Council a little time to resist the efforts some of us made to follow up the judge's invitation for the two parties to the action to meet and negotiate. I telephoned the Leader of Barnet Council, Councillor Richard Cornelius, and got a provisional date of 11 January for a meeting.

On Monday 3 January a General Meeting was held in the library for a plan of action to be discussed. Here are the minutes of this meeting, followed by Reema Patel's letter and a flurry of e-mails of 5 January between Reema, myself and Robert Rams, the councillor responsible for culture and the man who closed the library on 5 April 2012:

From: Keith Martin

Sent: 04 January 2013

Hi everyone

These are the minutes of the Meeting at FBL on 3 January 2013. I have taken the liberty of incorporating Phoenix's very helpful Notes for Draft Licence, which he explained to the meeting. Thank you for these, Phoenix.

Minutes of a meeting at Friern Barnet Library on 3 January 2013

1   PRESENT

Mark Weaver (facilitator)

John Moser JM

Keith Martin (minutes) KM

Lucy Nowell

Chris Bernstein

Dave Parker

Mike Bernstein

John Parker JP

Fiona Brickwood FB

Reema Patel RP

Frances Briers

Peter Phoenix PP

Pauline Coakley-Webb PCW

Poppy P

Fiona Cochrane FC

Alfred Rurangirwa

Sheri Darby

Barry Rawlings BR

Rosa de Souza

Yvonne Ruge YR

Barry Fineberg BF

Martin Russo MR

Tim Flitcroft TF

Anne Storey AS

Harry Gluck   HG

Diane Taylor

Maureen Ivens MI

Anthony Timmons

Emily Mc

Arun Mistry

and others

2   THE COURT CASE

RP reported the successful outcomes of the case, whereby the possession order for repossession of the library was deferred until at least 1 February 2013 in order to allow discussions between the Council and the community for the continuing use of the library thereafter.

3   LICENSEES

It was agreed that the community be represented in negotiations with Barnet Council by a group of volunteer licensees, and that these be:

John Moser, co-ordinator
Fiona Brickwood
Keith Martin
Anne Storey
one nominee of Save Friern Barnet Library Group

Perhaps further co-options would take place.

Agreed that RP would write forthwith to Barnet Council confirming the invitation for them to be represented in a first meeting with the licensees on 11 January 2013.

RP

The agenda would include such items as:

1   The redirection of Council funds towards FBL, made available by the Council's unilateral decision not after all to have a Landmark Library at artsdepot.

2   The revision of the Council's Library Strategy, formulated on 16 July 2011 and made out-of-date by the Landmark Library decision.

3 Co-operation between the Council's Arts and Libraries Departments and Friern Barnet Library for future events in the community.

4 Terms of the licence agreement.

PP suggested the following Notes For Draft Licence

Provisional discussion to be flexible and negotiable

1 To run library 5-6 days a week for the next 6 - 18 months.

2 To keep tidy and in good order

3 Council has responsibility for repair and maintenance

4 Council to pay utilities - Water-Heating-Electric-Internet

5 Council to provide funds a minimum of £20,000 -£50,000 and to pay for at least one librarian, with the support and back up of our pool of 50 community librarians (which includes 6 ex librarians)

6 As well as opening 6 days a week <u>11-7pm</u> also to provide community workshops and events.

7 We would be very interested to view a council proposal on points for license and to integrate some of our draft license points.

8   Council to cover public liability insurance

9   Council to assist with CRB checks for
        volunteers.

10   Council to provide link up to local and
        national library service.

He added that

We are beginning the process of setting up a
legal entity, possibly a not for profit company
limited by guarantee. We have a meeting
next Wednesday 9th Jan of our licensees
and will have our second license group
meeting on Thursday January 10th.

Once a licence has been agreed we see a transition
period whereby the library may not need to be
occupied overnight and can be opened and
closed by local community key holders. The occupy
London network will continue to help and support the
local community empowerment process that will
hopefully have saved this local library and
community centre for many people to enjoy for
generations to come.

BF and FB both advocated liaison with Community
Barnet (formerly Barnet Voluntary Service Council),
an umbrella organisation of some four hundred

bodies, in good standing with Barnet Council. FB to liaise with Victor of Barnet Community Council.

FB

HG made the point that the licensees must prepare a Business Plan.

PCW stressed that what is required is a seamless transfer to any new bidder occupant.

KM emphasised that the book stock should not be dissipated. It represented a major increase in the value of the library as a going concern.

MI suggested that in the eventuality of the Council enforcing removal of the books, that they be moved temporarily for safe keeping, perhaps at the nearby St John's Church.

TF and FC suggested research into the Localism Act for details of Neighbourhood Plans and Community Land Trust takeovers.

4   JUDICIAL REVIEW
Deferred.

5   COSTS Of APPEAL
Estimated to amount to over £600.

A collection at the meeting realised £143 plus a cheque for £235 and promises of donations which, thought RP, would be kept in a discrete Clients' account by the solicitors. RP

6   CLOSING WORDS

PP and RP congratulated everyone present for a positive concerted community spirit. Reema in turn was thanked for her leadership and enthusiasm.

KM
4.1.13

From: Reema Patel [mailto:reema87patel@googlemail.com]

Sent: 05 January 2013 11:38

To: cllrrobertrams@gmail.com; cllr.r.rams@barnet.gov.uk

Cc: Keith Martin

Subject: Friern Barnet Community Library - Negotiations and Meeting 11th January 2011

Dear Cllr Rams

I write in my capacity as a local community activist - I chaired a meeting on 3rd Jan 2013 at the library to determine the community library's response to the judgement at the Barnet County Court . This was attended by over 40 people and included members of the community, some bloggers, the Save Friern Barnet Library group, Friern Barnet Co-Action, members of the Occupy movement, councillors and a range of other interested residents. This group of attendees collectively agreed to form a legally constituted body for the purpose of temporarily running a volunteer library and to approach the Council to discuss a licence agreement to that effect for the next 18 months. Some individuals put themselves forward as prospective trustees/governors of this body.

You will receive notice by the 10th January of who the individuals responsible for this body will be and the form this constituted body will take.

I am writing to formally _ask you whether you will set aside time in your_ _diary to meeting with those individuals, or a smaller delegation of that_ _group on 11th January?_

I am also writing to address your concerns (included below this email) that discussing a licence would prejudice other possible community organisations who wanted to enter into a licence. There is nothing preventing you from entering into discussions about an interim licence at this stage. Neither is there anything to prevent you from entering into discussions with a body that will be formed by the end of the month.

Just to ensure we start off on the same page; after the hearing on 18 Dec the Council gave a legal undertaking to allow the defendants and others to remain inside the library until the end of this month.

Your statement that the defendants in the possession proceedings must leave before the end of this month before considering negotiating this licence with community groups is therefore in direct conflict with the legal undertaking not to enforce the possession order for a 6 week period. That period was given in order to enable the Council to enter into negotiations to ensure the continuity of that library. Your email therefore amounts to an outright refusal to negotiate a licence during this period.

The judge encouraged the Council to come to an agreement over the grant of a licence with members of the volunteer run library in that 6 week period. It is envisaged that the library would be run voluntarily as it is currently being run as an interim measure whilst the building would remain unsold for a period of 18 months (an interim licence) allowing other community groups to come forward to make their bid under the Localism Act 2013. The possibility of allowing a volunteer library to continue was a key reason for granting a 6 week period extension and legal undertaking in the first place - a legal undertaking that Barnet Council agreed to.

There is no reason for why discussions must take place only after legal constitution if it is clear that there is a body that is in the process of legally constituting itself and will be able to enter into a licence by the end of the month.

Furthermore I am not sure why entering into discussions at this stage would mean the giving of favouritism to one group over (at present, hypothetical) other groups. You are of course free to also meet with other groups who put themselves forward to run a volunteer library up until the expiry of this 18 month period but there are none yet that I can identify.

Mention of a prejudiced bidding process was only in relation to the community right to bid under the Localism Act 2013 which is a different matter altogether and not relevant to whether the Council might grant an interim licence to run a library up until the point the bidding process is concluded.

I can see no reason for why your meeting with members of the community who are interested in providing a valuable public service will mean you are giving favouritism to one group over another. If this was the case then no councillor or Cabinet Member would ever be able to meet with anyone. Certainly, the judge didn't seem to think this would be a problem.

I look forward to an open and frank discussion with you and other delegates on the 11th about how the Council and the volunteers can best keep a community library which is providing a valuable public service running for the next 18 months. As you are aware the building cannot be sold for a significant period yet. Please confirm that you will be able to meet with us then.

Best wishes,

Reema.

From: Cllr Robert Rams [mailto:cllrrobertrams@gmail.com]

Sent: 05 January 2013 07:53

To: Keith Martin

Cc: Robert Rams; Andrew Harper; Daniel Thomas; Richard Cornelius; <rosiecanning1@gmail.com>

Subject: Re: Dialogue

Mr Martin,

I will meet with all the groups that are interested in supporting a community library but your group must encourage the squatters to leave and form itself in to a fully constituted group.

At this time I am not going to give favouritism to one group and I look forward to all the groups coming forward as fully constituted groups with detailed plans.

I will make further statements on the issue next week as I must support all the groups that are now coming forward.

On 5 Jan 2013, at 03:07, "Keith Martin"
<keith.martin18@btinternet.com> wrote:

Dear Councillor Rams

You are quoted on Chris Hewitt's column on the Hendon and Finchley Times internet page as follows;

"We will happily talk to the real members of the local community," and again,

"We have been very generous in terms of agreeing to talk with them."

In this rather bizarre method of beginning our dialogue I have posted back:

"Dear Councillor Rams

It is good that you are willing to talk to the people in the Friern Barnet community who have high expectations of how you will be surprised and delighted to see what is being achieved in our library, when you come and see it for yourself. We are looking forward to our dialogue with you, and are confident that you, like everyone who comes into the library for any of the wonderful events being organized there, will realize that this vibrant addition to Barnet's many good libraries is something that you will wish to preserve and encourage. By all means look in at any time. There is no need to wait for the first meeting with the licensees on 11 January. If you wish to bring colleagues from Capita or the Cabinet, please do so.

Do get in touch. My phone number is 020 8445 7850.

Keith Martin, one of the licensees."

This invitation extends to all of you.

My initial contacts over Christmas were with Cllr Cornelius, to agree on a date for the first meeting with representatives of Barnet Council. We in the community have been hearing rumblings about the library portfolio being passed initially to Cllr Thomas, then in April to the Children's portfolio of Cllr Harper, but perhaps on 1 April to Capita. Hence my invitation to all of you, so that you may all see for yourselves what it is that we are talking about, so that the business plan being prepared by the licensees will make more sense to you.

I am sure we can reach a solution satisfactory to all of us. That is what the dialogue is about.

Best wishes

Keith Martin

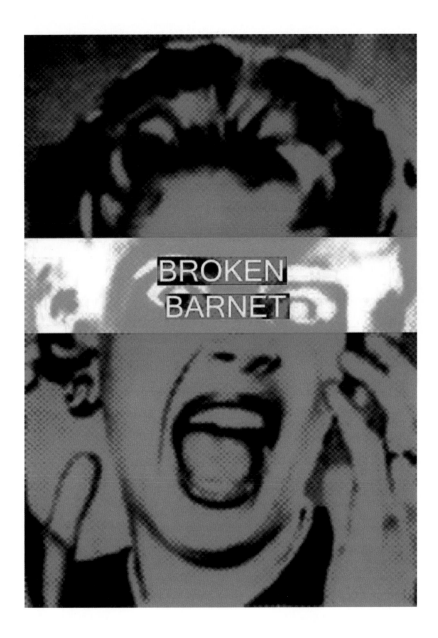

Tuesday, 8 January 2013

A betrayal of trust:
Barnet Tories, Robert
Rams, and the library
that will not die

Extraordinary news tonight.

*Updated Thursday: scroll down

Barnet Council, in apparent defiance of the judgement given at last
month's court hearing regarding the future of Friern Barnet Library,
has announced that it will hand over control of the building to a third
party, that is to say a charity, 'commUNITY Barnet', an umbrella
organisation of voluntary services in the borough.

According to the story in the local Times paper, as reported here by
Chris Hewitt:

"Barnet Council has invited a third party to take over Friern Barnet
Library, ending any chance of direct negotiations with the current
occupiers.

The local authority announced this afternoon it will hand a licence to CommUNITY Barnet, a charity supporting voluntary organisations in the borough, which will run the building in the interim.

The charity will take charge of the library until February and has been asked to co-ordinate community groups looking to take over the building in the long term.

The council will begin accepting community bids for the building in February and it hopes interested groups can come together and enter one unified application through the licence holders.

Libraries portfolio holder Councillor Robert Rams told the Times Series that it would be up to CommUNITY Barnet whether or not it chose to hold discussions with the library's current occupiers.

Friern Barnet Library was shut down in April as a cost-cutting measure by the local authority, which is ultimately looking to sell the property.

Squatters gained access to the empty building in September and have since helped a number of community groups set up their own library with a stock of more than 8,000 donated books.

Barnet Council won a possession order to evict the squatters in December but agreed to delay until the end of January while it held talks with the occupiers over giving them a licence to continue running the library.

Today's announcement means no direct talks will be held and Cllr Rams said it would be up to CommUNITY Barnet to discuss the continuation of the library with appropriate community groups.

He said: "The squatters will have to leave so we can take control of the building and have it to offer to community groups during the official bidding process.

"The squatters have made it very clear who they are and we will go ahead with the eviction at the end of January if they don't leave themselves.

"We have put in place a clear mechanism with which the council can work with the community – it is a great opportunity."

The news will come as a blow to members of the Friern Barnet Community Library who last week put forward five representatives to begin negotiations with the council.

The group had requested a meeting with Cllr Rams and council leader Richard Cornelius on January 11 but told the Times Series this morning they had received no reply to repeated email requests."

Unlike Cllr Robert Rams, Mrs Angry was in court for the two day hearing last month, in which Judge Pearl made it clear that possession of the building was to be delayed in order to allow negotiations in regard to a licence to begin.

The judgement was made in respect to the dispute between local campaigners and occupiers and the council. No mention was made of negotiations between the campaigners and any other party.

Rams' statement today would also appear deliberately to ignore the message sent by his own party leader in correspondence with leading member of the library campaign, Keith Martin:

On December 26th, Cornelius wrote to Keith Martin:

Dear Mr Martin,

Thank you for your email, which I have read. Now that the case is settled and subject to legal advice that dialogue will not prejudice any matter, colleagues and officers will be happy to discuss a proposal for a community library in the Friern Barnet area.

Happy New Year

Richard

The implications of Cornelius' email are perfectly clear: negotiations will take place between both parties, represented on behalf of the authority by 'colleagues and officers', not a charitable body, appointed by the council, upon which it relies heavily for funding.

Where is the accountability here? Where is the obligation to show transparency in the decision making process? Where is the democratic process?

An unelected, charitable foundation financially dependent on the local authority suddenly charged with responsibility for a building which is now registered as a community asset?

Mrs Angry understands that commUNITY Barnet may have its own interpretation of the role which it believes it has been given, and that this interpretation may differ somewhat from the picture presented by little Robert Rams, the man who, you must remember, has already brought us an invisible landmark library, and been obliged to be seen to campaign against the effects, in his own ward, of a parking policy already endorsed by himself and his Tory colleagues.

Oh - updated already ... Rams has just tweeted his own statement, via 'twitlonger': try not to laugh.

"A key part of my Friern Barnet Lib Statement today "I'd like to stress," said Councillor Rams, "that because of the success of the One Barnet procurement process we have more contractual savings than we expected and the council is in a different financial position than when we started our library review. We also have slightly less pressure on our capital budget which gives us the scope to look favourably on bids for the building from local residents."

What rubbish. Any 'contractual savings' are total fantasy: Rams is desperately trying to regain control of this story, dressing it up as 'looking favourably' at local bids.

The truth is the law obliges the council to consider local bids, and he knows it. If there is more money, Rams, do the right thing, and re open the library - support this branch, just as you have so enthusiastically supported your extravagantly subsidised enterprise for the millionaire Tory voters of Hampstead Garden Suburb.

Or maybe stop the deprofessionalisation of Barnet libraries which your philistine administration is in course of implementing?

Campaigners for Friern Barnet Library are very angry tonight: they feel that they have been betrayed, yet again, by their elected representatives. Who can blame them for feeling this way?

More importantly, perhaps, the point to be considered is how this latest development will be seen if and when the judicial review is under way.

Ultimately, of course, the real test will be in May 2014, when Robert Rams and all his shabby Tory colleagues must face the judgement of the electorate for every little shameful thing they have done in these last few years of what must be, by any standard, one of the most infamous Tory administrations in the history of modern local government.

This was Broken Barnet, in January 2013. How was it for you?

*Update:

Here is the full text of Rams' own release, which would appear to contradict his own statement to the Times: note that he says nothing about a licence to commUNITY Barnet, and says it is up to the charity whether or not it 'negotiates' with local campaigners, rather than that it must help them put in a bid ... also the council's intention to sell goes forward, and of course there is no guarantee that ANY community group's bid will be seriously considered ... confused?

Yep. All of it is a total mess.

"Below is a copy of the full press release sent out today regarding Freirn (sic) Barnet Library.

Community Barnet asked to support local groups interested in future of former Friern Barnet Library building

Barnet Council has asked Community Barnet to support community organisations seeking to make "Right to Bid" proposals for the former Friern Barnet Library Building.

Councillor Robert Rams, cabinet member for libraries said: "We have been able to support a very successful community run library in Hampstead Garden Suburb, in large part because local residents have a fully accountable and effectively organised body that we can provide with public assets.

"I'd very much like to see a similar body in Friern Barnet and Community Barnet seems perfectly placed to support groups of local residents in becoming properly established and able to develop a "Right to Bid" proposal. I understand that they have already had an approach from a potential group. Ideally we would only have a single bid but we could consider more than one."

As the next step in the Right to Bid process, the council will confirm its intention to market the building at Cabinet Resources Committee in February. Bids cannot be formally invited before that decision.

Any bid for the site would be bound by full planning and building regulations."

*Updated Thursday:

Incredible story now in the local Times:

http://www.times-series.co.uk/news/10153732.Third_party__will_not_run__library_following_squatters__eviction/

CommUNITY Barnet have denied Rams' story, and told reporter Chris Hewett that they wish only to help support any groups, including the current occupiers bidding to run the library:

"CommUNITY Barnet's CEO says the organisation has no intention of running the library in Friern Barnet despite suggestions it had struck a deal with the council.

Libraries portfolio holder Councillor Robert Rams had said the voluntary sector support group would be handed a licence to run the building until official bids were made.

But the charity's interim CEO Denise Murphy told the Times Series that no such agreements were made.

She said: "We were somewhat surprised. We had been asked if we would support the groups that want to run the library services in Barnet and we said yes.

"We didn't talk about a licence at all. We're an infrastructure group, we don't run services."
Squatters gained access to the Friern Barnet Road building in September and have since helped community groups set up their own library in there.

Barnet Council says it will evict the squatters at the end of this month before marketing the property on February 25.

Groups and businesses then have six months to submit bids for the council's consideration and the authority says its current budget will allow it to look favourably on applications from within the community. CommUNITY Barnet has been invited to support any groups wanting to submit a bid.

The organisation will also assist the current occupiers, or any other group, looking to continue the running of the library in the six months between the eviction of the squatters and the council's final decision.

Mrs Murphy said: "Should the Friern Barnet library groups or any other groups want to make a bid, we will be there to support them.

"There is no agreement with Barnet Council – they proposed it to us and we have said we will be open to any groups that ask for our help.

"We would of course have helped anyway as that is what we do. We had already had some phone calls from one or two of the current occupiers before the council approached us.

"We have only had one group in touch with us so far and that is the people in the library at the moment."

What an absurd situation. Note the significant detail in this report: the reference to marketing, after the occupiers are evicted. Rams claims community bidders will be considered - oh, because suddenly its current budget will allow it to look 'favourably' on such proposals.

What does that mean? Where has the extra allowance come from? Is this from the Landmark Library disaster? Is it enough to make a community bid more attractive than a bid from say, a supermarket, or a gym, or any other property developer? The law demands only that Rams & co consider the community bids. They will then be able to turn away and say sorry, but best value requires us to accept a higher commercial offer. And don't think our Tory councillors are not capable of such a trick: we've seen it all before.

Rams position on the library issue is surely untenable now: he has dragged a charitable body into a political controversy and caused even more antagonism over this contentious issue. Either he should give in with good grace, bow to the will of the residents of Friern Barnet and return the library to its proper place, properly funded and secure in the heart of the community - or he should resign.

Posted by Mrs Angry at Tuesday, January 08, 2013

9 January 2013 Eight directors and three advisers were appointed to the board of the new Licensees.

Minutes of the first meeting of the Licensees of Friern Barnet Community Library
at 12 Duchess Close, London N11 3PZ on 9 January 2013

1   PRESENT

John Moser (in the Chair)

Keith Martin (minutes)

Fiona Brickwood

Pat Caplan

Harry Gluck

Jeffrey Newman

David Parker

Reema Patel

Anne Storey

2   INTRODUCTION

The members present introduced themselves, and Reema gave a brief account of recent events and the functions of persons volunteering to be licensees. Basically it was the intention to apply to Barnet Council for an interim licence to run the reopened Friern Barnet library for a period of eighteen months commencing February 2013.

3   LICENCE VEHICLE

It was AGREED that a formal legal licence vehicle be formed, and that it be named

FRIERN BARNET COMMUNITY LIBRARY LTD (voting For 5, against 2, abstention 1)

It would be a non-profit making company limited by guarantee. John would deal with the formation. John

4   DIRECTORS AND ADVISERS

It was AGREED that the following eight persons be appointed directors:

Fiona Brickwood	Friern Barnet Pro Action
Pat Caplan	Finchley resident
Harry Gluck	Save Friern Barnet Library Group
and Friern Barnet and Whetstone Residents Association	
Keith Martin	Barnet Borough Arts Council
John Moser	local resident
Jeffrey Newman	local rabbi
David Parker	Enfield resident
Anne Storey	Friern Village Residents Association

and that three persons be invited to advise the directors, namely

Rosie Canning	Greenacre Writers
Reema Patel	legal adviser, and
Peter Phoenix	Occupy activist

AGREED that of the directors

John Moser be the Co-ordinator

Anne Storey Secretary and

Keith Martin Treasurer

5   OBJECTS, MEMORANDUM AND ARTICLES

AGREED that John should submit standard terms in the

application for registration

of the company. John

6   DRAFT LICENCE

AGREED that Reema and Fiona confer with Community

Barnet, Locality and any other

relevant advisers, and draft and circulate draft terms to

the licensees. It would be for a term

of eighteen months from 1 February 2013 until 31 July

2014. Reema and Fiona

7   LETTER TO BARNET COUNCIL

AGREED that John should write forthwith to Richard

Cornelius, Leader of the Council,

with copies to Bill Murphy, Acting Director of Libraries,

and Victor Modolu of Community

Barnet, asking for a first urgent meeting with

representatives of Barnet Council. John

8   DRAFT BUSINESS PLAN

This was discussed and Keith circulated the attached draft for consideration by the licensees.

It outlined the respective functions of three potential partners to the management of the library,

Barnet Council

Friends of Friern Barnet Library, as yet not reformed, and

Licensees of Friern Barnet Community Library

Licensees

9   GOVERNANCE, FINANCING AND MANAGEMENT

Discussion deferred to next meeting.

10   REPORTING TO THE COMMUNITY

There would be a meeting at Friern Barnet library on 10 January for all supporters.

Keith suggested that the opportunity be taken to ask supporters willing to become involved

in such activities as being volunteer librarians, running events and fund raising to form themselves

into the reformed Friends of Friern Barnet library. This suggestion could be put forward on

10 January. Licensees

11   TOWNSHIPS

Discussion of a letter received from Barry Fineberg was deferred.

12   LIAISON WITH HAMPSTEAD GARDEN SUBURB LIBRARY

Harry was asked if he would, perhaps in conjunction with Maureen Ivens, maintain a liaison
with them.   Harry

13   NEXT MEETING

15 January 2013, 5pm chez Keith at 148 Friern Park, N12 9LU tel 020 8445 7850.

KM

10.1.13

FILE COPY

**CERTIFICATE OF INCORPORATION
OF A
PRIVATE LIMITED COMPANY**

Company No. 8369031

The Registrar of Companies for England and Wales, hereby certifies that

FRIERN BARNET COMMUNITY LIBRARY

is this day incorporated under the Companies Act 2006 as a private company, that the company is limited by guarantee, and the situation of its registered office is in England/Wales

Given at Companies House on **21st January 2013**

N08369031H

Companies House

THE OFFICIAL SEAL OF THE
REGISTRAR OF COMPANIES

Friern Barnet Community Library

The People's Library

Friern Barnet Road, London N11 3DR

In September the local community and activists reopened Friern Barnet Library. Barnet Council had closed the library in April, despite strong opposition. The occupation of the library was a direct action that has highlighted the massive community support for Friern Barnet Library.

On Tuesday 5th February, at midday, exactly five months since the occupation began, the community took possession of the Friern Barnet Library. The local community – represented by the trustees of the library – are on the verge of agreeing a two-year lease with Barnet Council (LBB) to run the library with some funding.

Your library is not just a place to borrow books – we have more than 8,000 now! – it is a community space that offers free and low cost activities to all. We are open from Monday to Saturday, 11am to 7pm. All children's activities are run and supported by local volunteers who are CRB checked.

How to get involved:
-Come and meet us – we have organising meetings every Monday at 7pm.
-Make yourself heard – phone, email, text, and tweet.
-Sign up to help in the library – the library can only stay open if we all get involved! You could volunteer for a short shift or contribute in any way you can.
-Donate – ask inside the library for details.

Websites
 ➢ peopleslibrary.co.uk
 ➢ sites.google.com/site/savefriernbarnet library
Facebook
 ➢ https://www.facebook.com/Friern.Barnet.Community.Library
 ➢ facebook.com/savefriernbarnetliby
Email
 ➢ friernbarnetcommunitylibrary@gmail.com
Twitter
 ➢ @savefriernbtlib

THE ROOF AFTER A TEMPORARY REPAIR

REEMA, SARAH AND KEITH

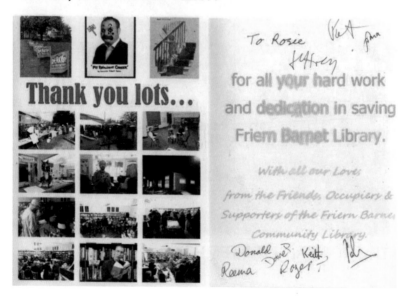

To Rosie

for all your hard work
and dedication in saving
Friern Barnet Library.

With all our Loves
from the Friends, Occupiers &
Supporters of the Friern Barnet
Community Library.

Barnet Spring March

March 23rd, from Finchley Central, 11 AM

Follow us: http://barnetalliance.org, @BarnetAlliance, #OurBarnet, #BarnetSpring

FROM THE TOP OF THE BUS

BLIZZARD AT BARNET SPRING MARCH

**SARAH SACKMAN AT FRIERN BARNET
COMMUNITY LIBRARY**

The occupation by the squatters on 5 September 2012 had seen the reopening of the library; a sudden and exuberant burst of activism which followed the sustained efforts of the Save Friern Barnet Library Group, which had been typified by good but essentially cautious organization.

The trial of 17/18 December 2012 laid the foundations of Barnet Council's transfer of ownership of the library to the community, which took place formally on 5 February 2013.

After the departure of the squatters, the months of February to July 2013 saw a reduction in the tempo of activity in the library. The self-styled trustees (the Charity had yet to be formed) lacked both the experience of the Save Friern Barnet Library Group and the flair of Phoenix and the squatters. They were therefore a prey to the dead hand of the Estates Department of Barnet Council who were intent on granting them a lease of two years, which would severely restrict their chances of obtaining significant Heritage Lottery Fund grants. Negotiations on the terms of the lease dragged on.

One sticking point was the repairs clause and the condition of the roof. Back in October there had been a small but persistent leak after rain, the drips in front of the toilet being caught in a bucket. This was reported to the Council, and eventually some workmen came and effected a temporary repair. This fell far short of the promise to put the whole library into a good state of repair before the signature of the lease, and the trustees deliberated how to ensure a fair resolution of the situation. In order to avoid any subsequent uncertainty over the condition of the roof upon the transfer, I held the ladder for a friendly Dutch occupant to take some photos on the roof, one of which is reproduced here. Mike Gee had earlier done likewise, to the serious detriment of his back.

Rabbi Jeffrey Newman had succeeded Pat Caplan as acting Chair of the Trustees, and bore the brunt of some difficult negotiations with Robert Rams.

Jeffrey had, in the headier days of November 2012, sent an e-mail from Hungary to the Council Leader, Richard Cornelius, on the subject of the Council's contentious One Barnet programme of massive outsourcing of contracts for public services. This is what he wrote on 18 November:

From: baps_active **On Behalf Of** Jeffrey Newman
Sent: 18 November 2012 05:05
To: Barbara Horn Jacobson
Cc: BAPS Active
Subject: Re: [baps_active] ACTION

"Though I am using a template and mechanism provided by others, this is my own, personal e-mail to you. Please read and consider it as such. I would appreciate a reply but, even more, I would so much hope that you will recognise the importance of the points raised.

I am deeply concerned, as a tax payer, voter, and Rabbi, that the One Barnet Programme of privatisation is being rushed through. The lack of transparency, the honest concerns of many of us and of Councillors who are NOT in Cabinet, increases my concerns behind our backs.

These few questions deserve deep consideration. Though complex and technical in nature, it is wrong to abdicate personal responsibility to the cabinet or council officers or to believe that those raising these issues are 'the usual suspects' or are motivated only by a selfish concern for their own jobs or political leanings.

We need you to feel confident that you understand the answers to these questions before you can vote with any conviction for or against the One Barnet Programme.

1. What model of privatisation is being implemented: Strategic outsourcing or Joint venture? Who changed the preferred approach and why? What are the risks inherent for each of these options? Have these risks been documented and planned for by the programme team and more importantly by internal audit, external audit and the Audit Committee? How confident are you as you read the risk assessment material?

2. How is delivery of service, quality, complaints and customer satisfaction going to be managed and by whom (monthly service reviews, measuring, escalations, reporting, punitive clauses in

contracts)? What influence will councillors retain under One Barnet regarding complaints?

3. How many jobs in total will be lost due to One Barnet? Of those jobs being outsourced to private companies, what percentage will stay in the borough? If Borough unemployment and hardship is increased, what will be the consequences?

4. Have you met any of the residents who are receiving services already outsourced to private companies? Should you not do some research?

5. Regarding IT systems, when changes and updates are needed because legislation, policies or the services have changed, how are these changes going to be paid for? Have you read the clauses in the contracts that clarify this point?

6. Have rigorous measures been put in place to restrict the private companies profiting from 'change requests' which incur additional costs or cuts in services?

7. What are the details of the contingency plans for the One Barnet changes? Even smaller programmes have a Plan B. It is professional and political suicide not to have one!

8. How, if this privatisation goes ahead, will it affect your role as councillors and the allowances you receive?

9. Have you, truly, a mandate to make these changes? If there were to be a Judicial Review, covering areas such as Public Consultation, due process, risk assessment, are you confident in the process?

Though it is true that this process has been underway for a considerable time, do you not feel under undue pressure to sign off huge and complex changes. These need to be put on hold and time given to allow for serious scrutiny. This should not be an ideological or party political issue. Have you read the background documentation as to what is happening in Cornwall? Have you fully considered the issues raised in reports by APSE?

It is not too late to stop and take stock and consider the implications of 'One Barnet' for the people you represent and the office you have been trusted to serve."

All good wishes and more thanks than I can possibly record...

Jeffrey

CHAPTER 12

9 FEBRUARY 2013   **SQUATNEY WICK**

We entered the secret world of this alternative community of squatters.

Young, international, very articulate and with astonishing and unexpected talents and skills of cuisine and delicate Spanish guitar playing. Outside, the walls of the buildings – former warehouses scheduled for demolition but graffitied with meticulously painted advertisements for forgotten household products in beautifully legible fonts.

How did we find this derelict warehouse? And how did the others in this audience for the world premiere of the short documentary film POLITE REVOLUTION - the story of Friern Barnet Library ? Eventually by receiving instructions by mobile phone from Phoenix!
It was just a very strange area, Hackney Wick, a lot of it scheduled for demolition.

My information about the film came from an e-mail from one of the squatters. This said that the film would be shown that evening at a squat near Hackney Wick station, and that instructions on how to get to the squat would be posted at the tube station. When we got there – I was with Fiona Brickwood - we looked for messages on lamp posts of which there were none. We walked round a bit, looking for the notices that weren't there, and asked a few people,

"Do you know about the world premiere of a film about Friern Barnet library?"

There seemed to be no numbers on the buildings or names of the occupants, after you had passed a long-closed pub next to Hackney Wick Overground (sic) Station. Street names, yes, and the very occasional fly-posted advert for a season of Polish films at The Cut. There were bright lights on in an incongruously chic club and restaurant, which one approached up the steep steps leading into another former warehouse. The waitress tried to guess for us where the destination of our film premiere might be.

This was Dickens's secret underbelly of London, largely unchanged since he explored this area and recorded the stories of life in *Oliver Twist, Great Expectations* and *Little Dorrit..*

CHAPTER 13

2013

A SERIOUS QUESTION

Evasiveness has long been a skill practised by politicians to avoid giving direct replies to searching questions. There is a battle of wits between questioner and politician, and the intellectual contest can be stimulating.

Nowadays this subtlety has been replaced, by many of the young councillors on Barnet Council who aspire to careers in politics, by a cruder, direct denial of the civilised rules of debate. At public council meetings, half an hour is sometimes set aside for questions. At a scrutiny committee to reconsider the closure of Friern Barnet Library, Cllr Brian Salinger posed some searching questions.

'Where in artsdepot would the Landmark library be situated?'
'When would it open ?'

Robert Rams, the Cabinet member responsible for culture, knew about the unpublished feasibility study, and could have given an answer – surely the purpose of the scrutiny? He chose instead to put in to bat a council officer, Bill Murphy, who gave an evasive answer which avoided Brian's questions. The Chair, instead of reprimanding both Rams and Murphy for failing to answer the questions, instead chose to criticise the public gallery for requesting proper answers. What a strange situation!

The story of Friern Barnet Library has served to illustrate an increasing unease among thinking people about the role of elected councils in managing local affairs, and about their performance as trustees of the interests of their constituents. Some councillors who used to work as public servants have changed their perspective to think of themselves not as servants but as masters.

These matters have been called into question by two recent legal cases and the judgments made by the judiciary.

1   The judgment by the judge in the County Court on 18 December 2012 to delay the enforcement of the eviction of squatters, to allow negotiations to take place between the
        Council and the community on the reopening of the library, was clearly influenced by the defending barrister's argument that the Human Rights Act gave rights of protest to the squatters. We use the term "squatters", but these were public-spirited people who achieved a positive result for the library and the community.

2   The judicial review brought by Maria Nash of Barnet Council's decision to outsource huge contracts for public

services to Capita brought forth the judgment that the Council decisions WOULD HAVE BEEN OVERTURNED but for the technicality that the complaint was not made within the short time limit allowed. The Council should take note of the essential decision of the judge and not rely on a purely administrative point.

These two judgments call into question the legality of the actions of Cabinet and individual councillors in taking decisions for which they have no public mandate or authority. That is clear from the manifesto upon which they were elected, which made no mention of outsourcing.

The councillors are trustees. A trustee has duties to the property of the trust, which are in this instance the assets of the citizens of Barnet, and to the manner in which they carry out the terms of the trust. What conclusion can be drawn about the failure of councillors to abide by their obligations as trustees? How on earth can they change the daily control of the assets of the trust without the authority of the citizens of the Borough?

There will undoubtedly be consequences.

CHAPTER 14

2014

THE FUTURE

The library was opened in 1934. This book is written seventy-nine years later, in 2013.

In negotiating a lease with Barnet Council this year for a continuing term, the trustees presented them with a Business Plan for our management of the library and, included within it, our vision for the long term; for the next eighty years. At least, that was how the draft left my pen. The Council chose initially to restrict its commitment to a lease of two years and included in its draft lease a term to this effect.

There was considerable debate among the trustees on the question of the duration of the lease, and on the details of the Business Plan; principally on whether or not to include as expenditure the cost of employing a co-ordinator/librarian at about £37,500 per annum, which would put total annual expenditure at around £60,000. I counselled an initial negotiating stance of an eighty-year lease and £60,000 annual expenditure.

The eight-strong committee favoured by seven to one a stance of acceding to the Council's offer of a two-year lease and an annual grant of £25,000 for each of those two years, with a possible extension of the lease at a later date if both parties were willing. The committee was less happy with the Council's proposal for the repairs clause which in their draft provided for the tenant to pay for repairs, and for the Council to put the building and roof into an adequate initial condition. The advice of Community Barnet, the former Barnet Council for Voluntary Service, was sought and listened to. They said that they thought the Council would not relent on the repairs question.

The fact that my views were overruled by the majority of trustees had the effect that this majority determined the composition of our negotiating team, on which I was not represented. My suggestion that they co-opt two experienced members of Barnet Alliance for Public Services to reinforce our strength, and Rosie's suggestion that I be drafted into our team, were both rejected. Rosie was an adviser to the trustees, but had declined an invitation to be one of their number.

The matters were discussed also within the wider circle of the "main meeting" of library sympathisers. This took place normally every Monday evening in the library, and which loosely provided a mandate for the trustees to follow in their negotiations with the Council. I was open about my views, to the point of circulating to one of the main meetings a written "minority report", and in writing letters which were frequently published in the Barnet Press, the Barnet Times and the Ham and High, the Hampstead and Highgate Express. One such letter contrasted the actions of Camden and Barnet Councils. Camden had granted a twenty-five year lease on Lauderdale House in Highgate, together with a grant of £350,000 and the support of the lessees' application to the London Heritage Lottery Fund for a grant of £800,000.

Thus there was tension between the negotiators for Barnet Council and those for the trustees, and an increasing realisation that the Council team had no brief to take decisions but in all respects reported back for instruction by the elected Council representatives, which effectively meant the Cabinet.

The further tension between the trustees and myself came to a head on 21 March 2013. At the beginning of this board meeting I was handed a letter from the other seven members, which I was invited to read and did so aloud to them all. The letter informed me that in applying for charitable status for FBCL they had decided not to put my name forward as a trustee "since it is quite clear that you are unwilling to adhere to the general agreements and consensus of the group." Attached to the letter was an Addendum of examples of my supposed inappropriate behaviour.

This letter was followed by a formal 21 days' notice of a resolution that I be removed from the Register of Directors. I was invited to prepare and present reasons why my membership should not be terminated, and to be accompanied if I wished by a friend to the next board meeting.

To cut this long story short Roger Tichborne, blogger of the Barnet Eye, and I duly attended this meeting, at which he made the point that it would be untrue to describe the board's action as being in the best interests of the charity, because it would be likely to have the reverse effect. The board nevertheless confirmed their action, but happily agreed to my request that neither side should publish any attacks on the other's conduct.

In truth the letter of no confidence came to me as a surprise; but its aftermath was a wonderful example of the capacity of human beings to support each other. Roger Tichborne and Theresa Musgrove – the redoubtable Mrs Angry, the scourge of councillors such as Robert Rams, Brian Coleman and the Leader Richard Cornelius – tore into the timorous actions of the FBCL committee, and came like avenging angels to my defence. Tim Flitcroft of Occupy and Aubrey Rose provided wise counsel. With such support my morale was restored, as was my determination to fight another day.

The story of the library since the Council Library Strategy was launched in July 2011 until the writing of this book in 2013 has already undergone a number of surprising and unforeseen somersaults.
In the context of our vision for the library over the next eighty years it is impossible to forecast its future, or indeed the future of any library or the continuation of printed books as a medium for education compared with the use of Kindles and no doubt other means of communication.

What a very strange world it is, and a strange contradiction in the attitudes of people towards helping their fellow human beings.

There are elected councillors in Barnet deputed by their colleagues to organize the cultural life for its 400,000 citizens, who close museums and libraries, and do not so much as visit a library that has been reopened by the efforts of the local community whom they are elected to serve.

And there are charities, one of them founded as long ago as 1679, whose aims for over three hundred years have remained to aid those in need. Miraculously, these charities can and do fill the gap left by the uncaring Philistine councillors. And who are the people who administer these charities; who decide which good causes should receive grants? Other local councillors, mostly. Funny old world.

But let me end this book on a positive note.

Friern Barnet Library has been saved from demolition by a Philistine and unsympathetic Barnet Council, despite their efforts to close it.

The community of Friern Barnet aided, it must be said, by the inspired and inspiring action of determined and dedicated squatters supported by the Occupy movement, has achieved a success in reopening the library and persuading Barnet Council to share a plan for its reopening and functioning as a public library, run by volunteers with professional leadership and guidance.

Long may it continue.

The final words come from Phoenix, as ever acting as a calm mediator and peacemaker, while other volunteers were getting embroiled in an ill-tempered argument about censorship of a film night at the library. Thank you, Phoenix.

From: Phoenix
Sent: 15 May 2013
To: Tim Flitcroft
Cc: Keith Martin

Subject: Phoenix appeal for cooperation re Film Night 3 May

Hi folks,

To keep community projects running takes a lot of love dedication and tolerance of a wide range of views.

Goodwill and a spirit of cooperation are needed, events of all sorts and volunteers are the life blood of any community centre.

My hope is that people can resolve their differences of opinion, draw a line under some issues and move forward.

This is essential to rebuild good will.

Hopefully there will be many more informative and interesting, community building film nights by donation.

The Occupy Economics working group is doing very important work envisioning better future financial situations and should be welcomed as a great contribution to the library or any community.

At these critical times for our environment, community and economy we must sometimes put aside the smaller petty view and see the bigger picture.

Cooperation is needed now, do not fall for the divide and rule pedalled by a few individual council lords.

The library campaign is something that has inspired many across the land, we must build on this victory, helping libraries and public services not just locally but nationally.

This is an appeal for cooperation across all those involved in the library picture,

Lets move forward in a positive way.

Love Phoenix

Keep networking

APPENDIX I

Second DRAFT

SCHEME FOR THE REOPENING OF CHURCH FARMHOUSE MUSEUM, HENDON, AND FRIERN BARNET LIBRARY

PARTNERS

London Heritage Lottery Fund

London Borough of Barnet

English Heritage

Arts Council England

Hendon and District Archaeological Society

Barnet Borough Arts Council

Society for the Furtherance of Critical Philosophy (SFCP)

New Carnegie Foundation

FUNDS PROVIDED BY

London Heritage Lottery Fund

London Borough of Barnet

...

TIMETABLE

Target

1   Meeting of representatives of the partners to
       consider the draft scheme, agree on any
       modifications and make plans for its implementation.
       30.11.12

2   Obtain agreement and cooperation of partners and
       prospective funding bodies.
       31.12.12

3   Plan the continuing management and funding
       of the Museum and the library.
       31.12.12

4   Agree a timetable for implementation of the Scheme.
       31.12.12

KM   23 .10.12

APPENDIX II

Friern Barnet Community Library

Draft business plan, 13 March 2013

1.   Summary

The present proposal aims to ensure the continuation of a library service to all Barnet residents in the present Friern Barnet Library building in close co-operation with Barnet Council and its libraries, broadening the activities offered therein to offer a community hub for the local population while playing its part in overall public library provision in the borough while contributing to community cohesion, engagement and self-reliance. Our proposal would develop the services provided so that the facility would serve as a model for the future, offering an example to other libraries in Barnet and beyond.

2.   Proposal

2.1 To work with Barnet Council and other interested parties to maintain a comprehensive and effective library service for the local neighbourhood of Friern Barnet in accordance with the 1964 Museums and Libraries Act; to develop the present Friern Barnet Library in its present location, largely managed by volunteers but in a Council-owned building. This would entail bringing in additional community activities and services, supported as appropriate by the library staff and by other local official or voluntary agencies and individuals.

2.2. To form a broadly-based community group to assist in policy and planning, staffing, organising and promoting community events, fundraising and outreach, strengthening links between Friern Barnet Library and the local community. These links would aim to provide services currently needed by the community. We would hope to use the services of CommUnity Barnet and The Royal British Legion to expand our access to volunteers.

2.3. To build on the proven track record of local groups in successfully liaising with the community and working imaginatively and creatively to enhance a successful library service at Friern Barnet Library, offering the widest possible range of community activities and facilities.

3.   **Mission and objectives**

3.1 Our mission is to reactivate the inspiration of 1934 when the library was opened; to rebuild the spirit of innovation with which it was created seventy-nine years ago, and to lay the foundation for its continued prosperous existence for at least a further eighty years; to become a truly community-based centre and library offering a variety of activities based on the needs and interests of the community of Friern Barnet which could become a model for other libraries and community facilities within the borough and beyond.

Our immediate objectives are:

3.2 to provide books for community use which accurately represent the reading tastes and needs of the adults of Friern Barnet; to provide books which inspire toddlers and schoolchildren to want to make reading an important activity in their lives; and to provide both serious and recreational reading for teenagers. This objective is in compliance with Barnet's stated ambition for us to 'create conditions for children and young people to develop skills and acquire knowledge to lead successful adult lives...'. The library services would include supporting and developing information literacy, providing access to ICT and giving support with ICT skills, and providing access to important information and services relevant to the local community;

3.3 to be a venue for jobseekers linking local businesses in search of apprentices with local "16- to 24-year-olds who are not in education, employment or training";

3.4 to be a venue for community consultation, discussion and engagement, thereby enabling active participation in local democracy and decision making;

3.5 to be a venue for community art and musical events with the aim of encouraging more local people to participate in these activities;

We are already providing much of the above: our intention is to expand our present community activities by reaching more of the population of Friern Barnet.

4.   History of the group:

Formed at the beginning of 2013 in response to the local authority's offer to negotiate a lasting settlement with a local representative entity, our trustee body is made up of a wide range of local residents and professionals representing residents' associations and voluntary groups including the Save Friern Barnet Library group, The Friern Barnet Co-action group, the Friern Village Residents' Association, The Friern Barnet and Whetstone Residents' Association and the Hollyfield Road Residents' Association, and supported by Friern Barnet Chapter of the Royal British Legion, local businesses on Friern Barnet Road, Queens Parade and Woodhouse Road and the wider community of Friern Barnet residents. We anticipate expansion of our membership to include all interested residents and users so as to engage the broadest possible cross-section of the local community.

5.   Current and recent services offered by library volunteers, free of cost:

- Library opening hours from 11am-7pm with no lunchtime closure as people need to access libraries at lunchtime.
- An internet service with help for those with few or no computer skills;

- A weekly mother and baby group run by a CRB Checked volunteer;
- A weekly toddlers' story and rhyme group with a CRB checked volunteer;
- Weekly adult yoga classes;
- French language classes;
- A venue for a weekly chess club for pupils and their teachers from the Dwight School;
- A knitting group;
- A-level Chemistry tutoring;
- "Meet the author" sessions;
- A comics workshop;
- Lectures on local history, political awareness, green issues and architecture;
- Talks on film making and photography;
- A meeting place for residents' associations;
- A meeting place for book groups;
- A toy library;
- A venue for creative writing classes;
- Lessons in cataloguing books and audio/visual material:
- Musical events;
- A memorial service for an elderly gentleman who relied on daily visits to the library before it closed.

6. Constraints on our project:

- **Money**: We have been given a start-up grant of £25, 000 with the possibility of obtaining a further £10,000 from Barnet Council from which we must find all the costs of our overheads, and the services of a paid caretaker and librarian/coordinator of volunteers. During the first 6 months we will further develop our business plan and approach sponsors and funders alongside our fundraising activities.

- **Lease**: Our lease of two years is positive in that we are charged a peppercorn rent, but a two-year lease makes finding grants difficult as grant bodies usually expect a five-year lease. We would seek to make the lease longer after the first year of operation.
- *Volunteers*: We need a very wide base of volunteers to ensure opening at advertised times. We are gradually getting there, but will continue to attach high priority to actively recruiting volunteers from the local community.

7. Management committee and staff:

- *Acting Chair*: Pat Caplan, Ph D Anthropology, Professor Emeritus Goldsmith's College
- *Acting Secretary*: Anne Storey, BA MCILIP, Research Librarian at Baker &McKenzie LLP (International Law)
- *Acting Treasurer*: TBA
- *Lease Negotiator*: (acting): Fiona Brickwood
- *Fundraising Officer*: Rabbi Jeffrey Newman
- *Press Officer*: Joanna Fryer, MA Classics, Head of Classics, Head of Careers and Teacher Governor, Finchley Catholic High, until 2005
- *Fundraising Team*: Sheri Darby, Janet Liversidge, Samar Baracat, James Dawson, Emily Marston- Cope, Frances Briers

- *Publicity*: Rosie Canning
- *Events*: Rosa de Souza
- *Volunteer rota*: Harry Gluck
- *Sponsorship*: Keith Martin, Chartered Accountant FCA, NALGO Chief Accountant
- *Caretaker*: Frances Briers
- *Website manager*: Dorothy Nichols
- *Schools liaison officer*: Maureen Ivens
- *Acting Librarian*: David Parker
- *Legal advisor*: Reema Patel

8. Management structure

8.1 We intend to follow the constitution used by many charities with membership paying a nominal sum which will provide members with certain privileges and voting rights. The management team will be partially replaced every year through annual elections.

8.2 We do not envisage a top-down management system but a community-led democratic system of elected officers to whom the various committees would report. These officials would be responsible for collating the activities of their group and reporting them to the wider group. They would be responsible for counting and banking any funds raised at their activities and for reporting events to the press officer. The committees are: fundraising, regular and special events, sponsorship, volunteer rota, book selection, website/newsletter, publicity, schools liaison, caretaking. Some of these committees will need large numbers, others will need only a few skilled people.

8.2 *Training*: We shall need CRB checks, health and safety advice, public liability advice, and training in cataloguing, purchase and issue of books.

8.3 *Key partners*: London Borough of Barnet Council Officers and CommUnity Barnet.
Key advisors: Locality.org.

8.4 *Recruitment*: We need a paid librarian/coordinator, especially a children's librarian, and a paid caretaker.

9. Services:

9.1 (See Section 6 for current services)

9.2 *Immediate future developments*:
- A venue for NEETS to meet prospective employers.
- A gallery for display of artistic, ethnic or historical projects.
- A regular meet-the-author event.
- A venue for visits from all local primary schools and a toy library for local nursery groups and families.
- A venue for AGE UK events.
- A venue for lectures, discussions and cultural events.

- A venue for invited youth bands at our regular Thursday evening open microphone sessions.

9.3 *Longer-term future developments*:
- Development of a summer festival on the Village Green next to the library.
- Development of an apprentice café using supermarket surplus in premises near the library. Profits to support the library.

10. Market:

10.1 There are 30,000 residents in Friern Barnet. We intend to reach out to the broadest possible range of the local population, in co-operation with local charitable, voluntary and community associations.

10.2 We want to establish regular use by and liaison with local primary and secondary schools to ensure that the Library continues fully to support education in the locality in line with the support shown by head teachers and other staff.

10.3 The community has enthusiastically come forward and donated well over 10,000 books (widely considered by users to surpass in quality what had previously been available) along with furniture and equipment. Our weekly open library discussion meetings are very well attended. We have a large list of volunteers who will help reach all the residents of Friern Barnet after a lease is in operation.

11. Competition:

We do not intend to compete with the Barnet Libraries, but rather seek to add to the range of library and community services available to residents of the borough. We will seek to provide more to our own community than was previously available: we would like, however, Council support in linking to an inter-library borrowing service so as to help our users access books we do not have and to offer a reciprocal service to users of local authority libraries.

12. Selling / PR

We intend to advertise our services in the local press and have events and services posters displayed in local businesses. We will use our own website for publicity and, after joining Barnet Borough Arts Council, we will have our events posted on their listings. We have an extensive email list for newsletters. We will also leaflet the local households with details of opening times and services and details of our website, as well as maintaining ongoing liaison with interested community bodies.

13. **Finance:** These are projections based on past spending by Barnet Council.

	Income	Expenditure
Donations	5,000	
LBB annual grant	25,000 Additional grant 10,000 Sponsorship 15,000 Fundraising 5,000	
Gas		3,000
Electricity		3,000
Rates		3,150
Water		150
Insurance (premises)		1,950
Insurance (public liability)		410
Telephone / internet		500
Postage		50
Stationery / consumables		250
Equipment		1,500
Building repairs / maintenance		4,000
Publicity		500
Kitchen / toilet items		200
Cleaning		2,300
Co-ordinator/librarian		37,500
Waste		300
Contingency reserve		1,000
Total	**60,000**	**59,610**

14. Sources of income:

14.1 Sponsorship

14.2 Grants: Locality.org and CommUnity Barnet are providing assistance with this.

14.3 Fines and photocopying: We are aware that Friern Barnet Library raised over £2000 last year from this source, but we do not believe that we would be able to match this; nor would such an approach be consistent with our community mission despite our willingness to raise financial contributions. Given the levels of deprivation in the locality we would not wish to be punitive, least of all in our early years of operation.

14.4 Membership: There is a suggestion that we might raise funds by asking for paid membership, but for the reasons outlined above this is highly unlikely to provide a large fundraising source.

14.5 Book sales: We anticipate cooperation with local bookshops and publishers to share profits at "meet the author" events.

14.6 Raffles, bake sales and bring and buy sales;

14.7 Designing and selling our own greetings cards with attractive pictures of the library.

14.8 Lettings: We have been approached by groups and individuals requesting to rent the library for a Vegan Banquet, concerts, tutoring, AgeUK meetings, art exhibitions and drama rehearsals. There would be a flat fee per artwork per month for art exhibitions. We could ask for £30 per hour for small group meetings and scale that up for groups of up to 100 people. For Sunday rentals we would ask £50 per hour for adult concerts but less for children's parties.

14.9 Future Fundraising events:

- Children's writing and art competitions with a small fee for entry.
- 200 Club.
- Pub Quiz fundraising nights in local pubs.
- Daytime hire for children's parties. (Sundays)
- Venue for surgeries eg police or Council.

15. Premises:

15.1 Opened in March 1934 as a then still rare purpose-built full-time lending library, Friern Barnet Library on Friern Barnet Road, N11 was designed by WT Curtis FRIBA, Chief Architect of Middlesex County and partially paid for by a grant from the Carnegie Foundation. It was maintained by Middlesex County Council until Barnet Council took it over in 1965. Its style is of a mock Tudor mansion surrounded by lawn, and it has been designated a Locally Listed Building of Historical and Architectural Interest and An Asset of Community Value. The building, approaches and fenced-off areas are altogether approximately 2000 sq metres. It was one of the first British libraries to have the open shelf system. (Prior to that people had to ask for the books they required). It has one main room with its internal walls lined with oak bookshelves and is well lit in daylight by enormous leaded glass south-facing windows. Clerestory windows light the east and north sides. It is designed so that ventilation comes in from behind the bookshelves to eliminate draughts on the readers. Its original oak parquet flooring is covered with grey carpet tiles. There are 3 doors-- large Cathedral-shaped double central doors to the front, an oak side door and a glass rear door. There are further swing doors inside the vestibule to prevent draughts. The front entrance has wheelchair access, and there is a safe slip road for dropping off readers and supplies. There is a small toilet and a sizeable kitchen. Behind the main room is a small room for storing supplies, and there are two closets in the main room for storage. There is a sizeable curved librarian's desk restricting access to the toilet and kitchen behind. There is a storage shed within the fenced-off rear approach to the library.

Outside there are gardens to the east and west. The west garden is awaiting the results of an independent inquiry to a neighbourhood application to list it as a Village Green. There were 600 local testimonies verifying its use as such by the community.

15.2 *Donations*: Of donated furniture are 4 computers, a printer, photocopier, 3 tables, six small wooden bookshelves, a coffee table, children's chairs and tables, 6 low mock-leather easy chairs, a librarian's chair, 6 stacking chairs and a dozen chairs for children.

15.3 **Needs**: We must accommodate 10,000 donated books so we need an extra 8 sets of metal shelves on wheels. To accommodate the computer needs of the community we need at least 6 computers with their own tables and a central computer printer. We also need a telephone, a working burglar alarm, a librarian's cart, 3 rotating paperback stands, six folding tables and thirty stacking chairs, a refrigerator, a flip chart and stand, six large conference display boards for art displays and a 'sandwich' board for announcing events to passers-by.

15.4 **Repairs**: Repairs needed are replacement wired safety glass in one of the swing doors (broken by a violent man from off the street), neon bulbs for two of the large neon lights, a repair to one of the blinds, return of the burglar alarm system and more Chubb locks on the front door as well as internal locks or keys to allow securing of staff and storage areas. .

15.5. **Future improvements**:
- We want to provide a handicapped toilet.
- We are looking into providing solar panels on the roof for the electricity supply.
- We would like to have a permanent gazebo for serving coffee and cakes in the rear courtyard.

APPENDIX III

2 May 2013   LETTER TO Cllr ROBERT RAMS

Cllr Robert Rams
London Borough of Barnet

2

May 2013

Dear Cllr Rams

Heads of terms for the lease of Friern Barnet Community Library

There is an important issue which I wish to raise urgently:

Clause 7   Term

Matters have transpired to bring to a head misgivings which some of the trustees have had since our negotiations began. I apologise for not raising the matter sooner.

Our recent quite successful ventures into meeting potential grant aiders have made us realize the necessity in most cases of having a long-term lease. The London Heritage Lottery Fund have given us good advice on this subject, as has Locality and the local Friern Barnet Educational Trust.

The recent very welcome news on 18 April of your granting a four-year lease on Church Farmhouse Museum, Hendon, to Middlesex

University, and of Camden Council granting a twenty-five year lease to Lauderdale House, have both reminded us of the disadvantage of Clause 7 as currently drafted.

I propose the deletion of "24 months" and its replacement by "twenty-five years".

If in your wisdom you prefer a term of eighty years, we should be delighted to agree with that. The library was built in 1934, seventy-nine years ago, and it conforms with our vision to be planning now for the next eighty years. A library is by definition a long-term project. The function of the trustees is to lay the foundation now for that long term.

If you wish to pass off this suggestion as coming from the Council, by all means do so. It is after all of equal value to the local community, whom the trustees represent, and the Council, who have a statutory obligation under the Libraries Act 1964 to provide a library service to the whole community, for Friern Barnet to get all available grants as quickly as possible.

We look forward to welcoming all councillors to join in the inspiring experience of the library, and I hope you will look in and see what is being achieved, with the cooperation of Barnet Council.

With all good wishes

Keith Martin. 148 Friern Park, Friern Barnet, N12 9LU

Tel 020 8445 7850